TEN LANDSCAPES

ROCKPORT

TEN LANDSCAPES
MARIO SCHJETNAN

EDITED BY JAMES GRAYSON TRULOVE

First published in the United States of America by:

Rockport Publishers, Inc.
33 Commercial Street
Gloucester, Massachusetts 01930-5089
Telephone: (978) 282-9590
Facsimile: (978) 283-2742
www.rockpub.com

Cover photo: Gabriel Figueroa

ISBN: 1-56496-857-X

10 9 8 7 6 5 4 3 2 1
Printed in China.

James Grayson Trulove is a book publisher and editor in the fields of landscape architecture, art, graphic design, and architecture. He has published, written, and edited over 40 books including, most recently, *The New American Swimming Pool, Hot Dirt Cool Straw, Ten Landscapes: Topher Delaney, Ten Landscapes: Michael Balston,* and *New Design: Amsterdam.* Trulove is a recipient of the Loeb Fellowship from Harvard University's Graduate School of Design. He resides in Washington, D.C. and New York, N.Y.

ACKNOWLEDGMENTS

The realization of this book is a long-held dream, since it exhibits two decades of work by my office, Grupo de Diseño Urbano to the American and international public. As such it is the opportunity to reflect and to acknowledge the persons who have supported and accompanied me in my exciting and arduous journey. First and foremost is Irma, my wife and companion for more than 25 years. Irma's role has been as a woman of love, understanding and unlimited support; she has been an intellectual companion with whom to share ideas, trips and perceptions. Our lives have been enriched by numerous voyages, places, and exhibitions and particularly by the marvelous persons we have met together. I also want to express my gratitude to our daughters Ana and Daniela, for their moral support and for bearing with a father who is obsessed by his work and continuously traveling, but who loves them deeply.

My recognition goes also to my father, Mario Schjetnan and my mother Margarita Garduño. With my mother I always had the marvelous feeling of being supported, even admired, and always loved. My father was an architect and I identified with him and his profession early in my childhood. But I also admired his sense of adventure, his love of nature and sports and his gentlemanly ways. We did not always share political views and that estranged us for some time but there was mutual respect and understanding which in the last years of his life brought us back together.

Another person I want to mention is my partner José Luis Pérez. We have worked together for almost 30 years. Sometimes a partnership is like a marriage: we have weathered together difficult times and learned to take advantage of our specific assets and skills to complement each other. José Luis has been a wonderful support, particularly during the times I have been teaching in the United States, at Harvard, The University of Arizona or The University of Pennsylvania.

This is also a pertinent time to recognize some of my mentors: Alvaro Sanchez and Ricardo Flores, outstanding teachers from the National University of Mexico; Donald Appleyard, Bob Royston and Garret Eckbo, enormous influences during my years at Berkeley; Enrique del Moral, Mario Pani, Max Cetto and Augusto Alvarez, Mexico's modernist masters who I had the good fortune to know in the 1970s and 1980s. But a very special place among those mentioned is reserved for Luis Barragan, with whom I had the privilege to be friends for almost 20 years.

The design professions are very much a collective art, like film or theater. You need a good team. In our office we have had the good fortune to work with young men and women of great talent and indomitable passion for their craft. It would be impossible to mention them all but I hope they can feel themselves acknowledged in these lines. My gratitude and recognition goes to them.

In every good work of architecture or landscape architecture there is a good client: an intelligent person or group of people who have visions, share dreams, and support the ideas, concepts and plans. We have been fortunate enough to have several such clients.

My appreciation goes to persons like Tulio Hernández, Delegate of Azcapotzalco, who had the original vision and determination to create the Parque Tezozomoc; Cristina Payan, our client for the Parque Historico Culhuacan and the Archaeological Museum in Paquime; Alejandra Moreno and Jorge Gamboa who supported the Xochimilco Ecological Park; Fernando Gomez Mayor of Aguascalientes; Holly Alonzo, for her vision of the Hacienda Peralta Historical Park Oakland; the courageous leaders of the Spanish Speaking Unity Council of the Union Point Park in Oakland; and many others.

We have collaborated with many architects and colleagues and I would like to mention a few architects Augusto Alvarez, Gonzalo Gomez Palacio, Enrique Norten, Felix Sanchez, and Jose Maria Gutierrez. My gratitude and respect goes to all of them. More recently, we have collaborated with colleagues in the United States, in particular Chris Patillo in Oakland and Chuck Albanese in Tucson. Finally, I want to thank The University of Arizona and specifically Dean Richard A. Eribes for his interest in and support for this book.

Partially funded by a grant from the College of Architecture, Planning, and Landscape Architecture, The University of Arizona

CONTENTS

LANDSCAPE, ARCHITECTURE, AND URBANISM

By John Beardsley

Mario Schjetnan is one of the contemporary world's most versatile and accomplished landscape architects, a cosmopolitan designer who is also emphatically Mexican. Steeped in pre-Columbian myth and colonial history, he has been shaped equally by an awareness of twentieth century art at home and abroad and especially by friendships with modernist designers such as Luis Barragan, Max Cetto, and Mario Pani. He has worked on a range of historic sites, from a pre-Aztec agricultural landscape south of Mexico City to the remains of a 10th century adobe city near Chihuahua. At the same time, he is no stranger to the punishing realities of modern Mexico, devoting much of his working life to the provision of housing and parks for the urban poor. He is familiar with the range of the country's ecosystems, from the rainforests of Chiapas to the deserts and high sierra of the north, which collectively make Mexico one of the most botanically diverse nations on the planet. Yet he has demonstrated the versatility to adapt his work to the increasingly global demands of practice.

One might say Schjetnan has building in the blood. His paternal grandfather came to Mexico from Norway at the turn of the twentieth century as a commercial attache; he stayed to help oversee the construction of a part of modern Mexico's infrastructure: the railroad from Guadalajara to Chapala Lake, where resort hotels were then being developed. The first Mexican Schjetnan was friends with the family of Luis Barragan and met the young designer when he was creating his first houses in Guadalajara in the late 1920s. Schjetnan's father was likewise a builder: an architect with a broad residential and commercial practice who also taught architecture for four decades, from the late 1940s to the late 1980s, at the National Autonomous University of Mexico (UNAM). Late in his life, he added landscape design to his practice—with a particular enthusiasm for golf courses—and helped establish Mexico's first degree program in landscape architecture at UNAM in the mid-1980s. Despite sharing a profession, there were stark differences between father and son. The elder Schjetnan came of age in an era when both art and architecture in Mexico were dominated by leftists—muralists such as Diego Rivera and José Clemente Orozco and architects such as Juan O'Gorman—yet he was not one of them. As a student, the younger Schjetnan would be drawn to precisely those artists and designers, and would ultimately take his first job in a public housing agency. In hindsight, Schjetnan credits his mother, Margarita Garduño, as much as his father with his scholastic development: "She was the intellectual in the family."[1] A graduate of UNAM with a degree in history (in the same class as Octavio Paz), she especially encouraged Schjetnan's interest in history, literature, and the theater.

Schjetnan studied undergraduate architecture at UNAM for five years between 1963 and 1968. He remembers the program especially for its enormity: there were some 6000 students at the time, divided into ten distinct ateliers. But he also remembers UNAM as an exciting place: he spent three years in an atelier directed by Ricardo Flores, who introduced him to the work of Louis Kahn, and Alvaro Sanchez, who taught him a great deal about construction. It was during these years that Schjetnan began to cultivate the broad interests that would later shape his practice. First, he immersed himself in Mexican modernist architecture: This was when he befriended Barragan, Cetto, and Pani. "I related to them more than to some of my instructors," Schjetnan recalls, "with the exception of Sanchez and Flores." Cetto's modernist credentials in particular were impeccable. He was a member of the Congrès Internationaux d'Architecture Moderne (CIAM); he knew Frank Lloyd Wright and Walter Gropius and had worked briefly with Richard Neutra; in the 1930s, he collaborated on several apartment houses in Mexico City with Barragan. Pani was known especially for his public work: the National Teacher's School in Mexico City and UNAM campus planning in the years just after World War II, and later housing projects.

Barragan's stature was more problematic at the time. Since receiving a solo exhibition at New York's Museum of Modern Art in 1976 and the Pritzker Prize in 1980, he has

been widely hailed in the United States as Mexico's leading 20th century architect. But
Schjetnan recalls Barragan was not especially admired by his professors in the 1960s. He had
trained primarily as an engineer rather than as an architect, which a few held against him.
Some thought him too closely connected with the wealthy, while others considered him too
much an artist rather than a functionalist. But it was precisely Barragan's belief in the artistic
dimensions of design that appealed to Schjetnan: "The thing I admired most about Barragan
was his attitude toward art. In every aspect of his life, he was a complete aesthete. . . I
learned many things from him: a special way of looking at life, the perpetual search for
beauty."

While Schjetnan was finding his own way into Mexican modernism, he was
acquiring an international perspective at UNAM. "Our generation was strongly exposed at
the National University of Mexico to two figures: Le Corbusier and Kahn." The emphatically sculptural approach of both architects remains important to Schjetnan; Kahn's Salk
Center is still for him one of the preeminent examples of a powerful architectural form that
is deftly integrated into its landscape. Schjetnan's education in Mexico was supplemented by
a summer trip to Europe after graduation in 1968, during which he saw—among much
else—Le Corbusier's work at Ronchamp and Marseilles; Breuer's UNESCO building in
Paris, with its garden by Noguchi; and a great deal of contemporary art in London and
Venice. He also encountered a world in convulsion: He entered Paris in June 1968 to find it
barricaded and occupied by tanks, and returned to Mexico City that August in time for
demonstrations that culminated in the shootings of hundreds of students by government
troops in October—events that solidified his social ambitions as a designer.

At the same time as Schjetnan was immersing himself in modernist architecture, he
was developing an interest in landscape. As a student, he scrutinized Barragan's landscape
projects: El Pedregal, Las Arboledas, and Los Clubes, among others. Barragan's adaptation of
traditional forms—stucco walls, water troughs, and cobbled pavers—to modern circumstances and his sensitivity to the spatial, material, and topographical features of his sites would
prove especially affecting to Schjetnan. Among his other inspirations were Roberto Burle

BELOW: *Aerial view of Chinampas, agricultural gardens, in Xochimilco.*

Marx and Lawrence Halprin: Burle Marx for synthesizing the language of European modernist painting, especially surrealism, with the climate and vegetation of the tropics; Halprin
both for the versatility of his practice—combining site planning, housing, urban design, and
landscape architecture—and for his formal language, derived from his understanding of natural processes.

Schjetnan had seen reproductions of Halprin's work in *Progressive Architecture*; he
was sufficiently impressed that he decided to attend graduate school at the University of
California at Berkeley in the fall of 1968 in the hope of encountering the designer in the
Bay Area. In fact, Schjetnan saw little of Halprin in California, though he took advantage of
the opportunity to study Halprin's work first hand. At Berkeley, he was exposed to acade-
mic notions then sweeping the field: systems theory, ecological planning, and techniques of
social inquiry including workshops and community meetings. Donald Appleyard was especially important, he remembers, in affirming the links for him between social research and
design. Again, however, Schjetnan made his own way. He was drawn to an older generation
of designers then in partial eclipse, notably Garrett Eckbo and Robert Royston. He spent a
summer working in Royston's office and remembers being one of only three students in a
studio with Eckbo, whom he describes as the first person to teach him that "landscape
architecture was a profession of design, a contemporary and functional design."

Schjetnan received a Master of Landscape Architecture degree in 1970 with an
emphasis in urban design. As he had attended Berkeley on a fellowship from UNAM, he
was required to return to the university as an instructor. He met his obligation by teaching
environmental planning—"the McHarg method," as he puts it—in the graduate division at
UNAM for two years. Then, despite his enthusiasm for landscape architecture, he took a job
as chief of design at INFONAVIT, Mexico's federal institute for worker's housing. He
would remain there for five years, from 1972 to 1977. "The first three years were fascinat-
ing," Schjetnan recalls, including extensive travel around the country and work with labor
unions on the creation of housing. "But I was not designing," he recalls. Schjetnan began
to take on private design work on the side, including some low-rise courtyard housing in

Mexico City. He eventually resigned from INFONAVIT in 1977 to open his own firm, Grupo de Diseño Urbano (GDU), in which the architect José Luis Pérez would become his principal partner.

Initially, GDU was run as a cooperative, on the model of an interdisciplinary collaborative workshop. But after Schjetnan took a management course while on a Loeb Fellowship at the Harvard Design School in 1985, the office structure changed. Schjetnan and Pérez divided responsibilities to express the way their different roles had evolved: Schjetnan assumed more of the conceptual design responsibilities while Pérez took on the greater share of project management, organizing production of design documents, resolving technical problems, and overseeing office administration and construction supervision.

Tezozomoc Park was the firm's first important project. Completed in 1982, it was a trial by fire. One of the largest cities in the world, Mexico City has long been beset by social and environmental problems of the first order, including an exploding population fed by migration from other parts of the country; extreme air and water pollution; and little accessible open space in the city's low income areas. These conditions have put intense pressure on politicians and city planners alike. Schjetnan was called by a delegate from the Azcapotzalco district, who wanted to convert an industrial site into a public park and a museum of the borough's history. At Schjetnan's suggestion, the park itself became the museum. Tezozomoc was designed to evoke the topography of lakes and mountains that characterized the Valley of Mexico at the time of the conquest; interpretive signs relate the political, cultural, and environmental history of the pre-Hispanic settlements that ringed the lakes. This is an inward-looking design—Tezozomoc is an oasis in a rough urban context. At same time, however, the project was linked with infrastructure needs. The lake was supplied with water from a treatment plant at an adjacent housing project, and the hills were created with fill from Mexico City subway construction.

The visible form of Schjetnan's work changed substantially after the completion of this park. While Tezozomoc's irregularly-shaped lake and undulating hills are somewhat isolated from their surroundings, later projects would take almost all their cues from the immediate visual and cultural contexts. And while Tezozomoc's language is suggestive of the picturesque, later parks would effectively blend historic forms with modernist idioms. Some aspects of the Tezozomoc project, however, remain crucial dimensions of Schjetnan's subsequent work: his sympathy for both cultural history and myth; his engagement with the social ambitions of design, especially the provision of open space in low income communities; and his attention to infrastructure needs, from water treatment to large scale environmental restoration.

Schjetnan's work at Xochimilco Ecological Park is perhaps the best example of his transformed design language and of his continued attention to social and environmental needs. The project involved two major components. One was the construction of a recreational and interpretive park of approximately 300 hectares, for which Schjetnan was the principal designer. The other, for which Schjetnan was an outside consultant, was the restoration of a 3000-hectare fragment of a pre-conquest landscape of agricultural islands made by the indigenous peoples of Mexico. Dating back to the 10th century, the network of islands and canals was declared a UNESCO World Heritage Site in 1987. All aspects of the project proved to be enormously complex: Technologically challenging and demanding a deft blend of urban and ecological design, the work also required protection of the site's historic character. At Xochimilco, Schjetnan says, "we finally had the opportunity to confront the last traces of the living myth. It was like entering a landscape of dreams, a living archaeology which had to be recovered, explained, celebrated, and conserved."

Ecosystem restoration was guided chiefly by hydraulic conditions: Polluted surface water was treated at new sewage facilities and large reservoirs were created to control stormwater runoff from the area's rapidly urbanizing edges. Eroded islands were recreated using meshes of logs filled with dredge and stabilized by willow trees. The project acknowledged this landscape's present-day productive and recreational functions along with its historical and ecological significance. Restored islands were returned to agricultural use and canals were dredged to reopen them to gondolas used by local families for weekend outings.

Within the park designed by Schjetnan, Mexico City's largest flower market was built; it is part of an interpretive landscape featuring demonstration plantings of trees and flowers like those farmed on adjacent islands. Park structures blend local materials with a simplified, geometric language characteristic of much modernist design. A stucco, stone, and tile visitor center, for example, is composed of a cylinder inside a cube; the building houses exhibitions on local archaeology, history and ecology. Nearby, cleansed water is discharged from handsome stone aqueducts into a 54-hectare lake that regulates water levels in the canal system, and an embarcadero was built to provide visitor access to gondolas.

Schjetnan's public parks are an expression of his long-standing ambitions for environmental justice; in this sense, they are an extension into landscape of his public housing work at INFONAVIT. By linking public space with infrastructure improvement, Schjetnan manages to find both the financing and the political will to provide recreational and open space for low income communities. Speaking of the neighborhood around El Cedazo Park, a project he completed in 1995 in Aguascalientes, Schjetnan told a writer for *Landscape Architecture* magazine: "This community is made up of the most marginalized people in Mexico...This park puts a stop to that marginalization and helps integrate these people into society." Noting that El Cedazo—like Xochimilco—combined a park and new infrastructure, Schjetnan insisted the effort at environmental justice was addressed "not by the park itself, but the roads and sewers as well. It's a question of urban rights."

Schjetnan's public works are typically executed on low budgets; they are correspondingly characterized by basic materials and modest detailing. Many suffer from poor maintenance compounded by political vagaries: A project supported by one administration might be neglected by the next. "We have learned to work with insufficient budgets, with scarce resources, with no continuity, and within a political time span of a president or a governor and, recently, with more public participation," Schjetnan explains. His park projects thus tell a cautionary tale about public work in the developing world. (Indeed, we have to look to his private landscapes to take the full measure of his skills with plants and construction detailing.) Yet Schjetnan has adapted. "We have learned to convince, to introduce not

only new ideas but a new profession, to instill enthusiasm and to supervise and fight and follow up on our projects to have them finished more or less as conceived." Schjetnan recognizes that much more is at stake than his own work or even the identity of the landscape architecture profession: He has come to see public space as crucial to developing cities. "In a context of rapid growth and change, as in Mexico or other Latin American countries, where instant cities can grow overnight, the permanence and certitude of designed open space gives direction and form to the city, a projection of the future. Urban open space—the void—is not the remnant of architecture but the spatial essence of the city, its form and its sense of being." These parks are markers of hope and fortitude notwithstanding their condition: Though they sometimes look tattered, they are soundly designed and can be restored. Meanwhile, they provide the spatial organization for an exploding metropolis.

While developing an idiom of contemporary landscape design attuned to historic, political, and environmental complexities, Schjetnan has also evolved an architectural lan-

BELOW AND MIDDLE: *The archaeological ruins of Paquime, Casas Grandes, Chihuahua.*
BOTTOM: *Xochimilco before restoration.*

guage remarkably responsive to landscape. The visitor center at Xochimilco, for example, doubles as a mirador: the flat roof affords elevated vistas over the lagoons toward distant mountains. At Parque de Mexico in Aguascalientes, buildings are stepped down the slope of a dam and double as terraces and a boat landing. But the best of Schjetnan's buildings engage in a still more intricate form of landscape interpretation. The Archaeological Museum of the Northern Cultures of Mexico at Paquimé in Chihuahua, for example, is partially recessed in an earthen embankment, diminishing the building's impact on the exposed desert site and its important pre-Columbian ruins. The berm also moderates the climate in the museum, sheltering it equally from hot summer sun and cold winter winds. Two courtyards in the museum introduce visitors to the plants of the Sonora desert and Chihuahua sierra ecosystems; a third is suggestive of an arroyo or dry wash and frames a view toward a distant mountain altar. The building sets a standard in Schjetnan's work for the effective combination of architecture and landscape in the service of environmental and cultural exposition.

It has become relatively commonplace in recent years to evaluate the work of designers outside the European and American mainstream in the frameworks of critical regionalism. The term, first used by architect Alexander Tzonis and historian Liane Lefaivre, implies a self-reflective adaptation or transformation of both modernist and traditional design languages.[2] As distinct from more superficially historicist or nostalgic design, critical regionalism employs the modernist technique of defamiliarization to reinterpret regional elements. At the same time, it uses a concern for local climate and topography as well as localized idioms of building to contest some of the universalizing assumptions of modernism. As a strategy, critical regionalism is contingent upon a process that Kenneth Frampton terms "double mediation:" a simultaneous critique and transformation of the broad spectra of local civilizations and of the global—and increasingly market-driven and consumption-oriented—culture that threatens to supplant them.[3]

Schjetnan professes considerable sympathy for critical regionalism and much of his work can be seen as an expression of its strategies. He typically finds his inspiration in the qualities of the environments in which he works: the climate, botany, and topography of the sites; the materials and building techniques of specific regions. Like Barragan before him, his work often involves reinterpretations of classic forms: plaza, alameda, cloister, patio. Schjetnan's landscape design is characterized by an acute and nuanced site interpretation that begins with specific ecologies. As Frampton affirms, critical regionalism "necessarily involves a more directly dialectical relation with nature than the more abstract, formal traditions of modern, avant-garde architecture allow," and Schjetnan's work does indeed represent what Frampton characterizes as "an engagement in the act of 'cultivating' the site."[4] But cultivating the site then extends beyond nature to the critical interpretation of regional histories and local artistic and economic traditions. The design for Xochimilco, for instance, embodies not only the site's restored ecology, but also its archaeological past and its subsequent transformation through agriculture and urbanization.

Schjetnan's respect for history as part of a living tradition has both poetic and political dimensions. He acknowledges an affinity to "magical realist" writers like Carlos Fuentes, Gabriel García Márquez, and Jorge Luis Borges, insisting they have "exhumed the myth and memory of places through their interpretive and creative elaboration of history." The meaning of a place, according to Schjetnan, "derives from these variables, and knowing both memories and myths allows us to connect the creation of place with a deeper being. . . this allows for the creative interpretation of history rather than the obvious evocation of signs and symbols that easily convert into nostalgic pastiche."[5] While exemplifying the poetic transformation of history, Schjetnan's work seems to imply that myth and memory retain their viability only in the context of contemporary environmental and social circumstances. This would explain Schjetnan's insistence on deploying historic form within a more pragmatic effort to alleviate vexing urban conditions.

Indeed, Schjetnan's work makes a great deal of sense within the context of evolving ideas about turn-of-the-21st-century urbanism. We now inhabit cities that are more appropriately described as metropolitan than as urban: that is, they are characterized by dense historic cores but also by sprawling peripheries, in each of which Schjetnan has labored.

The Dutch architect Rem Koolhaas has aptly observed that both parts of the metropolis are congested, though in the old centers the crowding is generally vertical, while in the margins it tends to be horizontal. Just as important, the recognition of congestion has led to an understanding that the various social groups inhabiting a landscape have different needs and ambitions for it. This understanding has consequences for landscape spaces at various scales. At the level of a park, it implies that design will be engendered through the superimposition in the same space of multiple, often competing programs; at the level of the metropolis, it requires the recognition of what Jean-Louis Cohen, writing about Koolhaas, calls "the coexistence of multiple, contradictory systems."[6] These contradictions are richly apparent at Xochimilco, to cite but one example. The park itself has to serve multiple programmatic purposes, among them employment, recreation, historic preservation, open-space protection, and ecological restoration. In turn, these programmatic requirements express the congested and contested character of the metropolis surrounding the park, where housing and recreational space are both in short supply; where unemployment is a chronic problem and where environmental stress is a terrible fact of life. While Schjetnan's work goes some way toward ameliorating these contradictions, it does not and can not eliminate them. Indeed, his work helps throw into relief the fact that conflict and instability seem to be the foundations of latter-day urbanism.

Among its many other achievements, Schjetnan's work helps provide us with the foundations of a new polemic for landscape architecture. His design is outwardly distinguished by a sympathetic recognition of the importance of landscape both to individual memory and to public history. His places have a past, he knows; but they will continue to create new memories. So they are shaped to be the locus of individual perceptual experience even as they recuperate history and address environmental and social needs. At a less visible level, however, Schjetnan's work argues for a new conception of metropolitan ecologies, in which architecture, urbanism, and nature all coexist in dynamic tension within a constantly changing mosaic. His designs reveal a concern both for form and for urban processes: that is, they exemplify a distinct aesthetic, but one that is generated in large part from underlying demographic, economic, and environmental pressures. His conception of landscape architecture addresses the practices of inhabiting the landscape as much as the ecology of habitat.

In the new metropolitan ecosystem, we might consider architecture as constituting the defining objects or patches, while the infrastructure of roads, communications, and mass transit provides the corridors between them. But landscape is the matrix in which it all takes form and is thus the most crucial element in the system, though it is generally undervalued. Schjetnan's work asks us to take equal notice of nature, even—and especially—in the metropolitan context. The attention he insists we pay to the urban landscape is bound to lead us into unfamiliar territory, involving the consolidation of design with infrastructure needs; the generation of more complex, adaptable, even contradictory programs expressive of social flux; and the creation of as yet unnamed hybrids of residential, recreational, and productive space. But if our goal is a landscape that aspires to some measure of visual power, social equity, and environmental sanity, then an engagement with new metropolitan ecologies, such as we encounter in Schjetnan's work, is crucial to our futures.

John Beardsley teaches in the landscape architecture program at the Harvard Graduate School of Design. He is the author of several books on art and the environment, including Earthworks and Beyond: Contemporary Art in the Landscape; Gardens of Revelation: Environments by Visionary Artists; *and,* Art and Landscape in Charleston and the Low Country.

1. Unless otherwise noted, quotations are from conversations with the author or from other unpublished remarks.
2. First used in 1981, the term receives fuller exposition in Alexander Tzonis and Liane Lefaivre, "Why Critical Regionalism Today?" *Architecture and Urbanism* no. 236 (May 1990), pp. 22-33; reprinted in K. Nesbitt, ed., *Theorizing a New Agenda for Architecture* (New York: Princeton Architectural Press, 1996), pp. 483-92.
3. Kenneth Frampton, "Towards a Critical Regionalism: Six Points for an Architecture of Resistance," in Hal Foster, ed., *The Anti-Aesthetic: Essays on Postmodern Culture* (Port Townsend, Wa., Bay Press, 1983), p. 21.
4. Frampton, p. 26.
5. Schjetnan, quoted in Deborah Karasov, "Xochimilco: Where Myth and Memory Meet," *Public Art Review* (Spring/Summer 1999): 21.
6. Rem Koolhaas' ideas about congestion, articulated in his book *Delirious New York* (New York: Oxford University Press, 1978), are explored in essays by Jean-Louis Cohen and Jacques Lucan in *OMA–Rem Koolhaas: Architecture 1970-1990* (New York: Princeton Architectural Press, 1991), pp. 9-19 and 33-41. Koolhaas's conceptualization of a park as a "cohabitation of a vast number of human activities on the site" comes in the description in the same book of his firm's proposal for Parc de la Villette in Paris (p. 89).
7. I draw the language of patch, corridor, and matrix from the writings of Richard T. T. Forman, especially *Land Mosaics: The Ecology of Landscapes and Regions* (Cambridge: Cambridge University Press, 1995) and *Landscape Ecology Principles in Landscape Architecture and Land-Use Planning* (Washington, D.C.: Island Press, 1997).

TEZOZOMOC PARK

Azcapotzalco, Mexico City

Tezozomoc Park is popular in several senses of the word. Located in a densely populated, working-class district of Mexico City, it is heavily used, especially on weekends, by people with little other access to public space. Commissioned by the borough of Azcapotzalco and built on a limited budget, it was also designed in a popular idiom, drawing on a familiar language of park design with particular reference to the history of central Mexico.

At the heart of the 30 hectare (75 acre) park, completed in 1982, is a lagoon that recreates the contours of the extensive system of lakes that once filled the Valley of Mexico; it is surrounded by low hills echoing the topography of the region. The historic lakes are long gone, filled by the relentless forces of urbanization; the mountains too are built upon. The park provides a physical trace or reminder of the landscape of the central valley in the years before the conquest. The effect is surprisingly familiar to those steeped in the English park tradition: the irregularly-shaped lake and undulating hills are evocative of the picturesque. Yet Tezozomoc is distinctly contemporary in its execution. It is built on a reclaimed industrial site; the mounds were made of earth from subway excavations; and recycled water—treated sewage from a nearby housing project—is used in the lake and for irrigation. The park itself was extensively reforested and there is a municipal nursery on the site which produces plants for use in the locality.

ABOVE: *The lake at Tezozomoc evokes the ancient landscape of the Valley of Mexico.*
OPPOSITE PAGE: *The park provides recreational space for a crowded district of Mexico City.*

ABOVE: *One of sixteen obelisks depicting the history and myths of pre-hispanic settlements in the Valley of Mexico, now Mexico City.*

At the appropriate places along the edge of the lake are small plazas with obelisks indicating the location of the pre-Hispanic settlements that once ringed the valley of Mexico. With the collaboration of a biologist, a poet, and a historian, texts were chosen for these markers that illuminate the history, mythology, and ecology of the region. A small island in the lake even features a replica of the famous bronze sculpture by Olaguivel that stands in front of the Supreme Court Building in the Zócalo in the center of Mexico City. The sculpture depicts an eagle with a snake in its mouth perched in a cactus, a reference to the Aztec legend that Tenochtitlán—now buried under the Zócalo—was founded on the site of such an apparition. The combination of water, vegetation, aquatic birds, and interpretive material provides a glimpse into the past for the residents of Azcapotzalco, many of whom are migrants from other parts of Mexico with little prior knowledge of the history of the central valley.

The park's interpretive functions are complemented by tennis and basketball courts, a bike path, a cafeteria, an open-air auditorium, and a gymnasium. Recreational facilities are kept mostly to the periphery of the park; the bike path is separated from pedestrian circulation by a change in elevation. The original park design was quite eclectic, combining some axial paths and allées with more serpentine forms. But as the plantings have matured, the landscape has become more unified under the canopy of an urban forest. Tezozomoc is testimony to what can be achieved in the public sector, even with a modest budget and recycled materials.

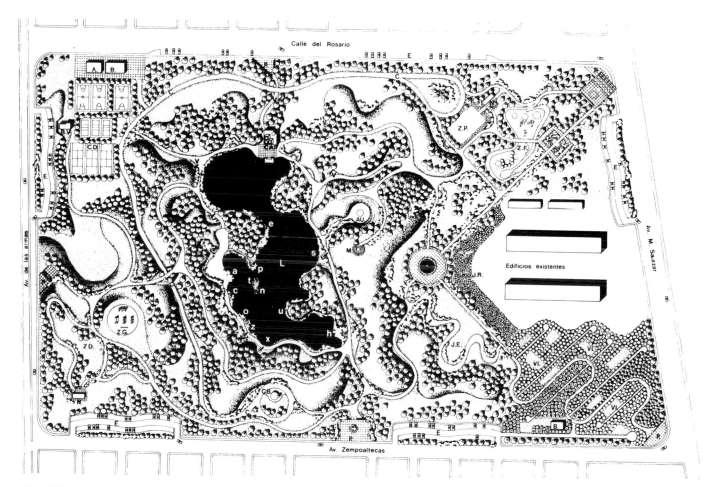

CLAVES

P.	Plaza de acceso	EM.	Embarcadero
E.	Estacionamiento	AU.	Auditorio al aire libre
A.	Administración	M.	Mirador
B.	Bodega	N.	Nucleo de servicios
C.D.	Canchas deportivas	Z.P.	Zona de patinaje
B.V.	Baños y vestidores	Z.F.	Zona de juegos infantiles
CA.	Cafetería	J.R.	Jardín de rosas

J.E.	Jardín de las esculturas
VI.	Vivero
C.B.	Caseta de bicicletas
C.	Ciclopista
Z.D.	Zona de días de campo
Z.G.	Zona de gimnasia
L.	Lago

Ruta Histórica

V.	Val e de México	O.	Coyoacan
e.	Ecatepec	z.	Tizapan
t.	Tlatelolco	u.	Culhuacan
a.	Azcapotzalco	x.	Xochimilco
p.	Tepeyac	s.	Texcoco
n.	Tenochtitlan	h.	Chalco
C.	Chapultepec		

ABOVE: *Tezozomoc includes this replica of a sculpture that represents the Aztec legend about Mexico City's origins.*

RIGHT: *Path leading to the food kiosk in the park.*

OPPOSITE PAGE: *As the park has matured, it has become an urban forest.*

RIGHT: *The park has attracted many social groups and activities.*

OPPOSITE PAGE: *Tezozomoc's lake is filled with recycled water; its hills were made of fill from Mexico City's subway construction.*

TOP LEFT AND OPPOSITE PAGE:
Formal in some areas, Tezozomoc is more picturesque in others
LEFT: *The park is enormously popular, especially on weekends.*
BELOW: *Pedestrian and bike paths are separated by a change in elevation.*

Malinalco House

Malinalco, State of Mexico

Built in 1985 as a weekend house for his family, Schjetnan's Casa Malinalco is one of his first and still one of his most convincing mediations between architecture, topography, climate, and cultural history. Malinalco is a village of small houses and narrow streets in a subtropical valley 110 kilometers southwest of Mexico City. Still largely agricultural, it is divided into eight barrios each with a small colonial church dating from the 16th or 17th centuries.

The L-shaped house was built on the gently-sloping, 1,100-square-meter site of an old orchard. Living room, dining room, and kitchen are aligned along one axis, bedrooms along the other, creating something akin to a traditional cloistered courtyard. Taking advantage of the moderate climate and establishing strong links with the landscape, the common rooms are designed as a covered terrace entirely open to the courtyard on one side. On the other, shuttered windows overlook a second garden. Each bedroom also has its own private patio in the back; still more outdoor space is available on the flat roof.

ABOVE AND OPPOSITE PAGE: *Water crosses a cobbled courtyard and collects in a small pool.*

ABOVE: *In the south garden of the house are the remains of an old orchard.*

Heavily planted along its perimeters, the courtyard is paved at its center with long narrow cobblestones that create a geometric pattern. This patio is crossed by a small rill connecting a stone basin with a square reflecting pool adjacent to the living room. A bold pink wall faces one side of the garden; the color was selected by Luis Barragan, who felt it was necessary to set off the muted colors of the landscape. Below the house are the overgrown but still productive remnants of the orchard, including coffee, banana, mango, and citrus trees. Farther down the slope are surviving agricultural buildings, including a horse barn.

In a climate that includes rainy and dry seasons, the landscape is designed to minimize both runoff and irrigation. Cobbled pavers allow percolation of storm water; runoff passes through the orchard to an absorption well near the barn. Grey water from the house is recycled into the orchard through a sand filter.

With its simple lines, spare detailing, and Barragan colors, but with a plan suggestive of Spanish or Moorish cloister gardens, Schjetnan's Casa Malinalco is an eloquent combination of modern and traditional design, at once urbane and respectful of its village setting.

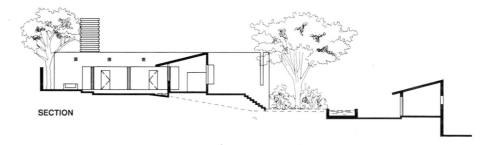

SECTION

GRAPHIC SCALE
0   1.00   5.00 M.
    0.50   2.50

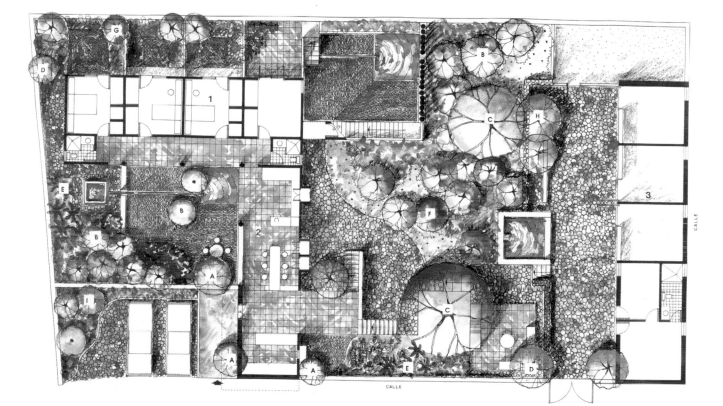

ABOVE AND OPPOSITE PAGE: *Views of the pool in the paved courtyard.*
RIGHT: *The orchard is irrigated with grey water from the house and rainwater captured in the pool.*

RIGHT: *One wall of the house was painted pink at the suggestion of architect and friend Luis Barragan.*
OPPOSITE PAGE: *The open-air living room is adjacent to the pool.*

ABOVE LEFT: *The L-shaped house frames two sides of a courtyard.*
LEFT: *The dining area and kitchen.*
BELOW: *The dining area, looking toward the living room.*
OPPOSITE PAGE: *View of preexisting orchard from the dining room.*

Mexican Cultural Center

Toluca, State of Mexico

Like his own house in Malinalco, the Mexican Cultural Center gave Schjetnan the opportunity to develop the connections between architecture, topography, and history, but this time on an large scale and in a public context. Completed in 1987, the Cultural Center was developed by the government of the state of Mexico on the 180 hectare site of a former hacienda west of Toluca, the state capital. The project encompasses a Museum of Modern Art, a Museum of Popular Culture, a Museum of History and Archaeology, and the main State Library, all set within a state park. It is adjacent to two universities, one public and one private, thus forming part of the capital city's most significant educational and cultural district.

Grupo de Diseño Urbano was responsible for the master plan for the entire park, for the landscape around the museums, and for the design of two buildings: the museums of modern art and popular culture. The museum campus is unified around a large concrete and stone plaza. A sequence of stepped platforms that stretch out over 250 meters, the plaza is on a north-south axis with a view toward the snow-capped peak of Nevado de Toluca. The plaza features a composition of standing volcanic stones in a large fountain, which gives the space the character of a ceremonial center. The hacienda's existing granaries and barns were adapted to become the popular culture museum, housing a large collection of crafts. The museum is organized around a central courtyard that features another large fountain; many of the museum's buildings also incorporate patios.

ABOVE: *Lobby of the Museum of Modern Art.*
RIGHT: *Isometric drawing of the Museum of Modern Art.*

The design of the Museum of Modern Art—a collaboration with Gonzalo Gomez Palacio Architects—was perhaps the most challenging aspect of this project. An unfinished, cone-shaped planetarium had to be incorporated into the plans. The planetarium was redesigned as an auditorium; exhibition spaces were placed around it; and a lobby, coffee shop, and bookstore were incorporated into the rest of the existing structure. The auditorium's exterior was surrounded by a set of concentric louvers that spread up and outward from the building; they sift natural light falling into the ring of galleries while seeming to levitate the cone. In order to reduce the visual impact of the whole structure and to link it with the truncated conical shapes of the volcanic landscape, the museum was partially concealed inside a berm which is in turn encased in a stone wall. Three elliptical excavations in the berm let additional natural light into the exhibition spaces. Schjetnan would later repeat this basic formula of a bermed, concentric construction at the Archaeological Museum of the Northern Cultures of Mexico, but with greater success: There, he would be unconstrained by an existing structure.

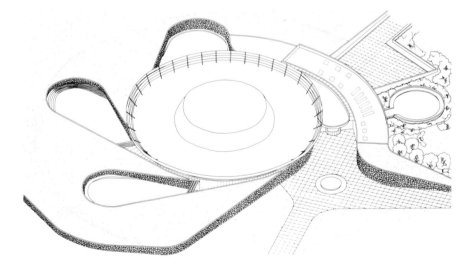

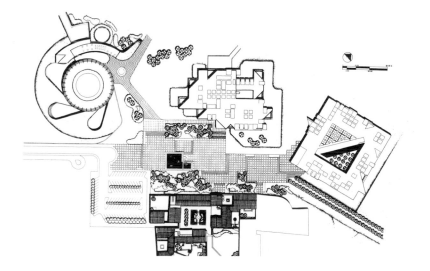

ABOVE: *The master plan for the entire park.*

LEFT: *The cultural center complex, with the Museum of Modern Art at the left.*

BELOW: *The plaza fountain.*
OPPOSITE PAGE: *The Museum of Modern Art is partially buried by a berm and ringed by a stone wall.*

LEFT. *Volcanic stone mural by Luis Nishizawa.*

OPPOSITE PAGE: *Entry into the Museum of Modern Art.*

FOLLOWING PAGES, LEFT: *Interior courtyard of the Museum of Modern Art.*

FOLLOWING PAGES, RIGHT: *View of the Nevado de Toluca Mountain from one of the interior courtyards.*

Culhuacan Historical Park

Iztapalapa, Mexico City

ABOVE: *This rendering by Brian L. Rothman suggests the site's appearance prior to the Conquest.*
OPPOSITE PAGE: *The reinterpretation of the original spring and water spout.*

Located in southeast Mexico City, Culhuacan Historical Park is adjacent to a 400 year-old former monastery, San Juan Evangelista, perhaps the best preserved 16th century monastic structure in Mexico City. The building is now the Culhuacan Community Center and houses exhibitions of local history and architecture. It is part of the National Institute of Anthropology and History, which sponsored the restoration of the landscape, completed in 1988.

The site was once on the edge of a lake, and the remains of a pre-Hispanic embarcadero built upon by Spaniards are still visible adjacent to the monastery. The design used these ancient walls to frame a pool evocative of the vanished lake. Fragments of a colonial-era stone aqueduct were reused to provide water for the pool. On a newly-constructed raised platform between the water and the exposed monastery walls is an area for cultural events, including a stone-lined performance space surrounded by steps. Along another side of the pond is an area for passive recreation shaded by willows.

The simple palette of stone walls and pavers and the use of basic geometric forms creates material and formal continuities with the existing building. The different levels separate different programs, but they also evoke the archeological character of site. At about one hectare (2.5 acres), Culhuacan Historical Park is one of Schjetnan's smaller projects. But his attention to the topography and history of this site was important in the development of later, more ambitious works such as the Archaeological Museum of the Northern Cultures of Mexico in Chihuahua.

BELOW: *Steps and platform leading
into the 16th century monastery.*

LEFT: *Amphitheater and stage, set against the monastery's wall.*
BELOW: *The site plan.*
FOLLOWING PAGES, LEFT AND RIGHT: *The archaeology is fully integrated into the new park.*

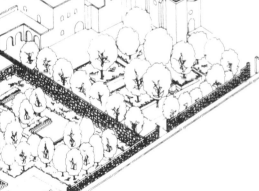

RIGHT AND FACING PAGE: *The park has become an oasis for the community within the surrounding dense and chaotic urban fabric.*

LEFT AND FACING PAGE: *The park is organized around small outdoor rooms defined by stones recovered from demolished buildings in Mexico City.*

XOCHIMILCO ECOLOGICAL PARK

Xochimilco, Mexico City

Xochimilco Ecological Park in Mexico City and the larger landscape of which it is a part are a powerful demonstration of the ambition and complexity of contemporary landscape architecture. An instance of environmental restoration on a vast scale, the project also addresses challenges of urbanization in one of the most populous cities in the developing world, providing both open space for recreation and productive land for economic development. Moreover, it does all this on multiple scales, from pedestrian circulation in a flower market to the workings of an extensive ecosystem.

Xochimilco, meaning "the place where flowers are grown," is a fragment of a pre-Conquest, even pre-Aztec, landscape of artificial garden islands created in the lake that once filled a large area in the valley of Mexico. The islands, called *chinampas*, were constructed by piling soil on reed mats and anchoring their edges with salix trees. Dating to the 10th century, this landscape of canals and rectangular islands was declared a UNESCO World Heritage site in 1987; the designation prompted a large-scale environmental restoration project undertaken by Mexico City and the borough of Xochimilco. Designed in the late 1980s and completed in 1993, the project encompasses some 3000 hectares of surviving islands. Schjetnan was the landscape architecture consultant on the ecosystem restoration project and principal designer of an approximately 300-hectare park within it.

ABOVE: *Aerial view of gondolas and the open-air stage.*

The site presented extraordinary challenges. Many of the islands were sinking from numerous nearby wells feeding on aquifers. Increased storm water runoff due to urbanization was causing additional flooding. Surface water was contaminated; canals were choked with pollution-loving plants. Those islands deep in the canal system were hard to reach and thus unavailable for agriculture; those nearer the edges were being encroached upon by unauthorized buildings. Thus the design for the environmental recovery project was guided by hydraulic strategies: water was pumped back into the aquifer to stabilize the site; large reservoirs were created to retain storm water; polluted water was processed at two new treatment plants. Cleansed water is now discharged into a 54-hectare lake created to regulate water levels in the canal system. Eroded islands were recreated using meshes of logs filled with dredge and stabilized by salix trees. (About 250,000 trees were planted during construction). The islands were then returned to agricultural use. Some have pastures for grazing; others are planted with flowers and vegetables. A vast tree nursery was located near the site; it produces trees that are then planted throughout Mexico City. Canals were cleared of harmful vegetation and rehabilitated for recreation as well as agriculture. Today, pole barges ply the canals of Xochimilco, especially on weekends; gondolas and gondoliers are available for hire at embarcaderos built around the edges of the site. Out in the canals, you can collect sustenance for body and soul: kitchen barges sell food, while others ferry professional musicians, ready to serenade visitors with patriotic and romantic songs.

At one edge of the chinampas landscape is Schjetnan's 300-hectare park, with different zones emphasizing natural, recreational, and interpretive features. Water again provides the basis for design in the park. The terraced entry is focused on imposing stone-lined aqueducts that discharge clean water into the new lake; the plaza also features a water tower in the form of an Archimedes screw. A visitor center completes the entry complex; it includes an auditorium and galleries with exhibitions relating to the region's ecology, archaeology, and agriculture. A roof terrace affords vistas over the lakes and canals toward distant snow-covered volcanos. From the entry area, a 400-meter pergola leads to an embarcadero, past an arboretum and flower beds representing the productive activities dispersed across the larger landscape. The remaining park area includes active recreation space with playing fields and ball courts; wetlands to collect storm water runoff and to provide habitat for aquatic birds; and demonstration agricultural zones in the recreated chinampas. To enhance economic activity on the site, the largest flower market in Mexico City was built adjacent the park's main highway approach. Its 1800 stalls are arranged on 4 x 8 meter module; the market covers some 11 hectares and is fully leased and very busy, especially on weekends. In all, the park is a microcosm of the regional landscape, highlighting its ecological, historic, agricultural, and recreational attributes.

The planning and construction of Xochimilco Ecological Park required extensive collaboration among designers, historians, biologists, engineers, and community groups. Thanks to their collective efforts, a degraded landscape has been transformed into a model of social renewal and environmental recovery. More than just a park to look at, Xochimilco is a working landscape.

ABOVE: *The roof terrace at the visitor center provides sweeping views of the park and surrounding wetlands.*

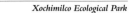

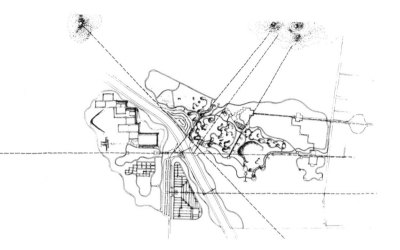

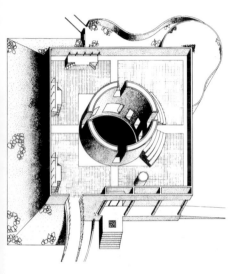

ABOVE: *Isometric view of the visitor center.*

TOP RIGHT: *Visual alignments to the mountains.*

RIGHT: *Xochimilco Park is organized into three different functional zones: the ecological park and lake, a sports park, and the plant and flower market.*

OPPOSITE PAGE: *Entry plaza with visitor center.*

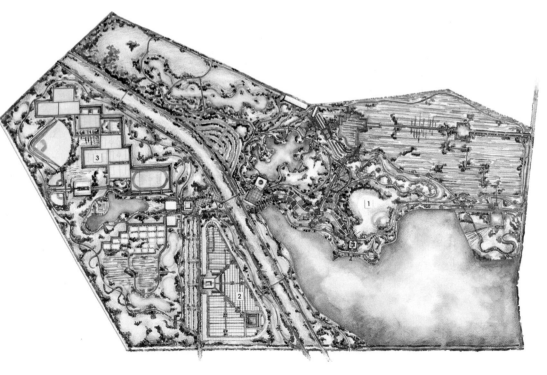

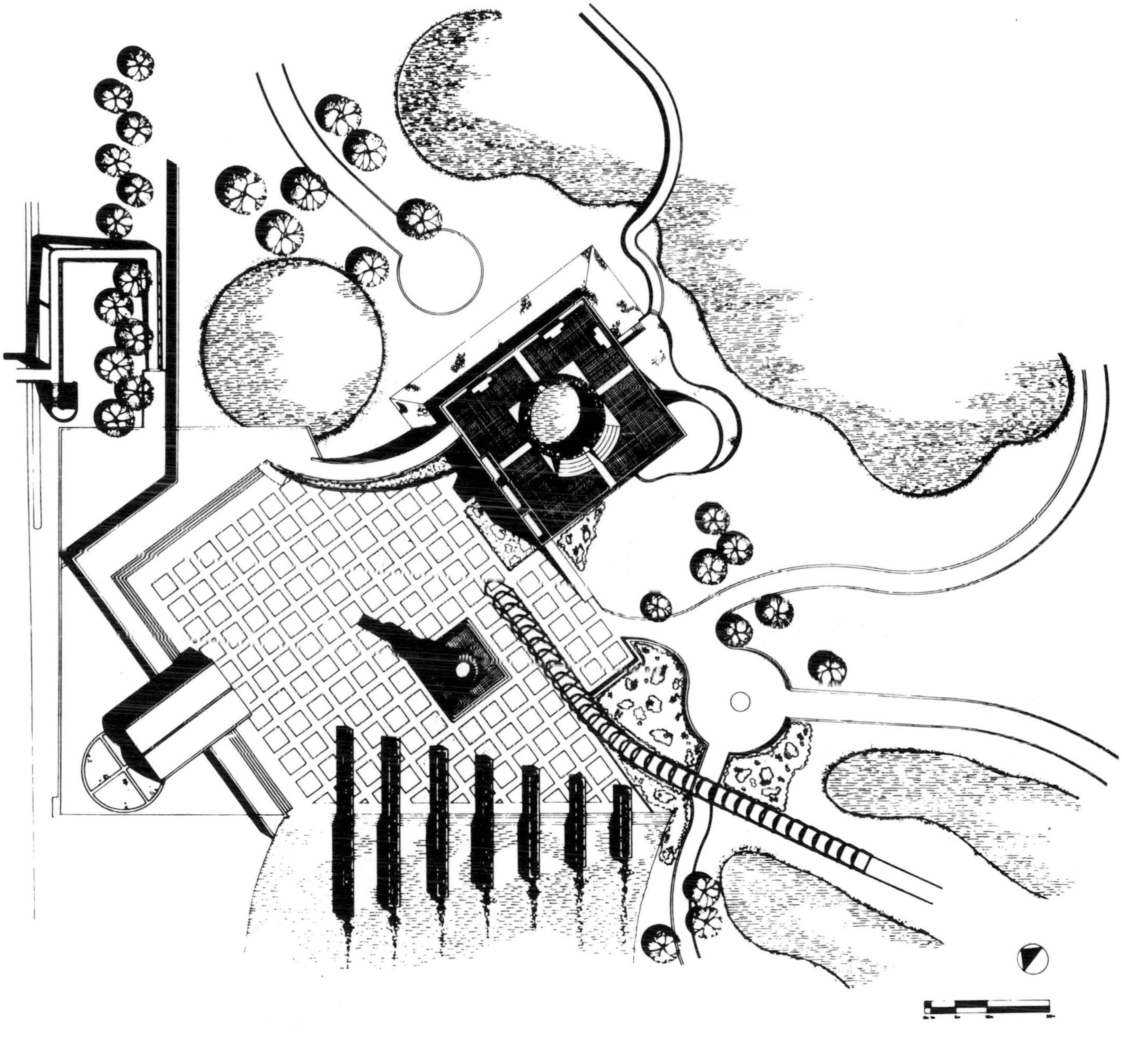

RIGHT: *View from the entry plaza.*
OPPOSITE PAGE: *The park includes Mexico City's largest flower market.*

ABOVE LEFT: *View of water tower from visitor center.*

LEFT: *Aquaducts release recycled and cleansed water into the lake.*

BELOW: *Restored wetlands provide diverse habitat for birds.*

OPPOSITE PAGE: *Entry plaza with water tower.*

BELOW: *Interior plaza and pergola.*
OPPOSITE PAGE: *The pergola passes demonstration plantings of flowers grown commercially in the area.*

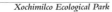

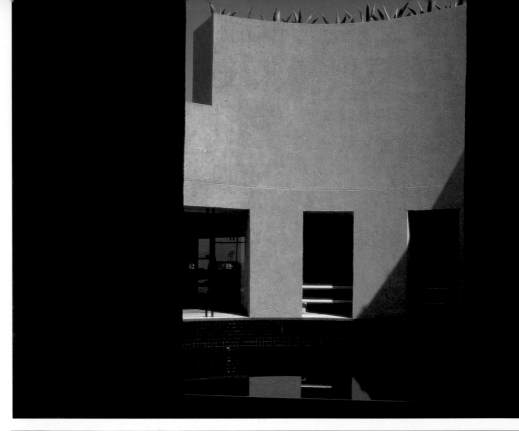

ABOVE RIGHT: *The interior courtyard of the visitor center is mirrored in the reflecting pool.*
RIGHT: *The rooftop of the visitor center is planted with aloe cactii.*
OPPOSITE PAGE: *The flower market includes 1800 modular stalls.*

MALINALCO GOLF CLUB

State of Mexico

Schjetnan's work at the Malinalco Golf Club ranged from broad-stroke planning to detailed design. His principal contribution is found in the Club's entry sequence, which includes a large square vehicular plaza behind massive stone walls, adjacent to shops and a pedestrian plaza that he also conceived. Schjetnan was additionally responsible for the design of streets and parking; he collaborated with master planners and golf course architects on the contours of the course itself and on the locations of lakes, cart paths, and service areas. He designed at the smaller scale of individual landscape features and recreation areas, orchestrating walls, waterfalls, and plantings, especially near the main club house and tennis courts.

Completed in 1993, Schjetnan's designs for the Malinalco Golf Club draw on several distinctive features of the regional landscape. The club lies in a lush agricultural valley surrounded by high cliffs, one of which boasts a pre-Columbian temple and fortress complex. The terraced landscape around Malinalco is divided by a network of dry stone walls that define individual property holdings. Consistent with this vernacular tradition, native stone was used extensively at the club for walls and street surfaces; indigenous trees and

ABOVE: *Dry stone walls (tecorrales) recall the surrounding agricultural landscape.*

other plants well-adapted to the subtropical highlands were planted along the roads. The detailing in the streetscaping is particularly effective: Small pavers make a solid surface for vehicles, while larger stones mark the medians and street edges. Trees are planted directly in the stone margins, shading the street. To the side, dense plantings of flowering shrubs provide a visual buffer between the street and golf course. A similarly fine level of detailing is found around the clubhouse and tennis courts. Stone walls divide gardens from children's play facilities; they also form small waiting areas near tennis courts. Grass steps and stone risers surround one of the courts, providing extensive if informal seating for those watching the matches.

Perhaps the most imposing feature of Schjetnan's work at the club, however, is the entry plaza. It is cut out of an imposing wall that steps downhill along the public road; purple metal gates lead to a 33 by 33 meter court with concentric pavers and a stone fountain at its center. Walls framing the entry plaza and fronting the street were constructed from massive boulders unearthed during golf course construction. At once ancient and modern in character, the plaza recalls the great scale of pre-Columbian construction even as it evokes the spare geometries of Luis Baragan's now largely lost compositions of volcanic stone, metal gates, and fountains at El Pedregal in Mexico City.

TECORRAL DE PIEDRA

FUENTE ESCULTORICA   PLAZA

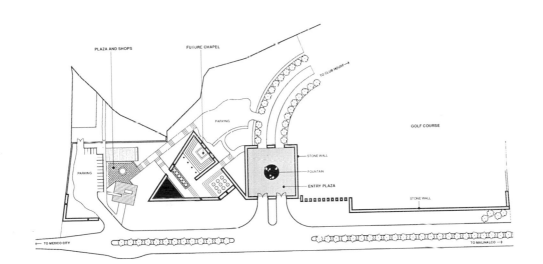

PLAZA AND SHOPS   FUTURE CHAPEL

TO CLUB HOUSE

PARKING

GOLF COURSE

STONE WALL

FOUNTAIN

PARKING

ENTRY PLAZA

← TO MEXICO CITY   TO MALINALCO →

STONE WALL

0   50   100 m

TOP LEFT: *View of lake, club house, and golf course.*
MIDDLE LEFT: *Section through entry court.*
LEFT: *Entry plan showing location of court, future chapel, and walls.*

ABOVE: *Detail of cascade.*
LEFT: *Entry median and stone walls leading into the golf club.*

LEFT: *Past the entry plaza, the views open up to the golf course and the valley.*
BELOW: *View of cascade and man-made lake.*

BELOW: *Stone terraces provide seating around tennis courts.*

BELOW: *Gates and pavers in the entry court.*

FOUNTAINS

Ofininas en el Parque, Monterrey, Nuevo Leon
Grupo Nacional Provincial, Coyoacán, Mexico City

Work at Oficinas en el Parque corporate buildings in Monterrey, Nuevo Leon, was completed in 1999. Landscape elements include an entry plaza, gardens, and fountains, which knit together two slender office towers. The plaza is paved with irregularly-cut local stones and features a fountain of tilted marble slabs of various sizes; lights and jets are set into a concrete base. Surrounding plantings are composed primarily of cactus native to the region. The fountain's slabs are quarried from a stone similar to that which forms the mountains visible from the site; together, marble and cactus are intended to evoke the character of the region.

The main garden is organized around a reflecting pool that forms a podium for one of the towers. Taking advantage of the sloping site, GDU designed for this pool an imposing curved retaining wall that doubles as a cascading fountain. The garden is planted with oaks and framed on two sides by a yellow stucco wall.

BELOW: *Entry plaza with native plants in Oficinas en el Parque.*

The corporate complex for **Grupo Nacional Provincial,** completed in 1994, is located in the redesigned and reconstructed buildings of a university campus damaged in an earthquake. Grupo de Diseño Urbano was retained by Augusto Alvarez Architects to create a plan for the landscape spaces between the buildings, which are connected by porticoes.

The principal open space at the complex contains a water feature that is interesting both from design and engineering perspectives. The client required a cooling system for the computer equipment concentrated in one of the buildings. The original engineering scheme called for a visually intrusive tower some 36 feet high. Schjetnan's solution, which was constructed instead, consists of two basins with 112 water jets about six feet high and a capacity of 640 cubic meters. The jets cool the water, which is then piped inside to cool the air in the building.

While functioning as part of the air conditioning system, the fountains also mask urban noise and provide a pleasant outdoor gathering space for company employees. The space is nicely detailed: platforms, seating walls, and walkways reminiscent of Schjetnan's work at Culhuacán are made of Santo Tomás chipped marble and float above the water, which is surrounded with cobbles of pale river stone.   Existing clusters of cedar trees were incorporated into the design and complemented with simple massed plantings of evergreen shrubs and roses.

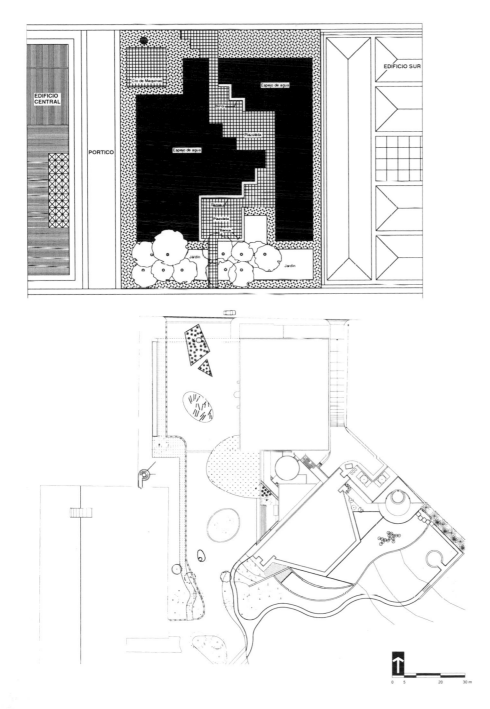

LEFT: *Plan of main courtyard fountain in Grupo Nacional Provencial.*
BELOW LEFT: *Plan of Oficinas en el Parque.*
BELOW: *View of courtyard fountain in Groupo Nacional Provincial from surrounding arcades.*

ABOVE AND RIGHT: *Detail of Ocotillo and Yucca desert plants in Oficinas en el Parque.*

LEFT: *Circular bench accomodates workers from the office towers at lunch.*
BELOW LEFT: *View of Ocotillo garden from main lobby.*

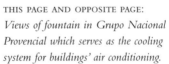

THIS PAGE AND OPPOSITE PAGE:
Views of fountain in Grupo Nacional Provencial which serves as the cooling system for buildings' air conditioning.

ARCHAEOLOGICAL MUSEUM OF THE NORTHERN CULTURES OF MEXICO

Paquimé, Casas Grandes, Chihuahua

Paquimé, at Casas Grandes in Chihuahua, is the most significant archaeological site in northern Mexico. Built beginning around 700 AD and abandoned in the mid-14th century, the city was a center of the pre-Columbian culture that stretched from the desert regions of Chihuahua and Sonora into the southwestern United States. Located in a wide basin with expansive views toward the Sierra Madre, the site is noted for extensive remains including pyramids, ball courts, platforms, kivas, and multi-story, rammed-earth houses. It also has yielded numerous artifacts, especially pottery, jewelry, and carvings. At the instigation of the National Institute of Anthropology and History, Grupo de Diseño Urbano was retained to design a museum adjacent to the site. The building was intended to house the collection of artifacts, interpret site history, and explain strategies for research and preservation at the ruins.

Design was guided by the strong, simple geometries of the historic structures and by the extreme—yet extremely fragile—qualities of the desert environment. The result, completed in 1995, is as much landscape as architecture. Organized around a large circular courtyard open to the sky, the building is half buried in a berm planted with desert grasses

ABOVE: *A rectangular court that resembles a dry wash looks out toward distant mountains.*

and cactus. While diminishing the building's visual impact on the exposed site, the berm also provides the museum with some shelter from blazing sun and dust storms in summer, cold winds in winter. Exterior walls blend with the colors and textures of the desert: curved surfaces are faced in local, rust-brown volcanic stone; planar elements are made of buff-colored concrete.

Entry to the museum is gained by crossing a broad stone plaza and descending wide stairs. Inside, exhibition spaces surround the central patio, while three smaller courtyards of different shapes and themes introduce natural light into the galleries and create a transition between the building and the larger landscape. The first is a circular patio planted with Sonoran desert plants; the second a triangular court with pines evocative of the Chihuahuan sierra; and the third an elongated rectangle suggestive of an arroyo or dry wash that frames a view toward a distant mountain altar. Flat roofs on top of the exhibition space provide additional views over the archaeological site and its expansive surroundings; the roof is accessible from the central patio or the entry plaza.

Visually discreet, the building is a remarkably sensitive intervention in a culturally and environmentally delicate context. It suggests the extent to which contemporary architecture might further both topographical and historical interpretation.

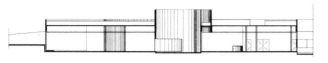

CORTE LONGITUDINAL 1.

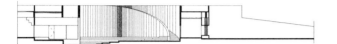

CORTE LONGITUDINAL 2.

CORTE LONGITUDINAL 3.

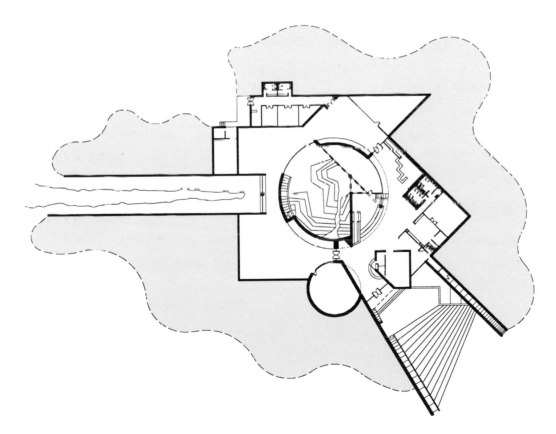

BELOW: *The museum's central patio is open to the sky.*
OPPOSITE PAGE: *A circular court evokes the landscape of the Sonoran desert.*

BELOW: *To minimize its visual impact on the exposed archaeological site, the building is mostly buried in a berm.*

BELOW: *The museum's central patio is open to the sky.*
OPPOSITE PAGE: *A circular court evokes the landscape of the Sonoran desert.*

BELOW: *To minimize its visual impact on the exposed archaeological site, the building is mostly buried in a berm.*

BELOW: *Rooftop terrace and staircase that leads to the central courtyard.*

TOP RIGHT AND RIGHT: *The design of the museum was the result of a close collaboration among the curators, exhibit designers, and architects.* OPPOSITE PAGE: *Entry plaza and ramp leading into the main lobby.*

Parque El Cedazo/
Parque Mexico

Aguascalientes

Schjetnan's Grupo de Diseño Urbano has been involved in the design of three parks in Aguascalientes, a small industrial city in a semi-arid basin in central Mexico. All three involved some measure of environmental restoration. The first was created on the site of a former airport; the two more recent—El Cedazo and Mexico Parks—reclaim historic earthen dams and constructed lakes (presas) that were once part of the city's water supply system. In addition, the newer parks are significant social amenities, providing open space along with cultural and recreational facilities in neighborhoods dominated by low-income housing. Both too, are part of larger infrastructure systems. Constructed with state funds set aside for water treatment and flood control, the two parks incorporate sewage treatment plants and help control stormwater runoff upstream of the city.

The dam at El Cedazo (the filter) dates back to the 16th century. By the 1950s, it was abandoned and the basin was polluted by sewage and choked with silt and trash. Schjetnan's work at the 28 hectare site, completed in 1995, involved the restoration of both the dam and the lake. It also resulted in the creation of a smaller body of water upstream from the lake, where trash that is washed down the seasonal streambed can be collected. Sewage from nearby housing projects is treated before reaching the lakes and the reclaimed water is used for irrigation in the park.

At the entrance to El Cedazo, marked with a bright yellow tower, is a cultural center. Composed of eight brick and glass pavilions with vaulted steel roofs, the cultural center includes facilities requested by community groups: a library, a child care center, and workshops for painting, music, dance, and adult education. The buildings are organized around two plazas and connected by a continuous portico. The balance of the park is divided

ABOVE: *View of restored dam and cafeteria building in Parque Mexico.* OPPOSITE PAGE: *Entry plaza and water tower in Parque El Cedazo.*

among zones of intensive use—basketball courts, cafeteria, boat dock, playgrounds, and picnic facilities—and more tranquil grassy areas planted with lacy, horizontal mesquite and pepper trees contrasted with opaque, vertical Italian cypresses. Walking and biking trails circle the lake; a chain link pergola, covered with bougainvillea, provides shade where the paths cross the dam. The overflow structure beside the dam doubles as an amphitheater and a rollerblading and skateboarding arena.

Parque Mexico, also constructed in 1995, follows the same basic plan as El Cedazo. It is also organized around an old dam and a restored lake, commonly called Presa los Gringos for the 19th century American and British industrialists who built it to provide water for a long-vanished textile mill. Public facilities in the 15 hectare park include a cafeteria and boat rentals; they are again concentrated in buildings near the entrance. These structures are more topographical in form than those of the cultural center at El Cedazo: they were conceived as terraces and stairs with views out over the lake. Paths circle the water; walled terraces with pergolas punctuate the trails. A road crosses the dam in this instance, knitting together two previously divided neighborhoods. Indeed, social and environmental conditions around this park were even worse than those around El Cedazo. Adjacent to the site was a gaping quarry-turned-landfill; a squatter's settlement had grown on its margins. The empty basin, as at El Cedazo, was watered chiefly by sewage. Creation of the park coincided with closure of the landfill and construction of new housing and a water treatment plant.

Given challenging social contexts and budgetary constraints, Schjetnan aimed for elegant if restrained design strategies in these parks: minimalist geometries; low-cost but attractive materials such as glass block, colored concrete walls, and stone pavers; and spare but effectively varied plantings. Combining environmental remediation with cultural facilities, these parks are as much social as natural environments. They suggest a contemporary conception of the park not as an escape from urban infrastructure but as its extension into open space. More poignantly, they are an expression of faith in the conviction that landscape architecture can be a significant agent in social improvement.

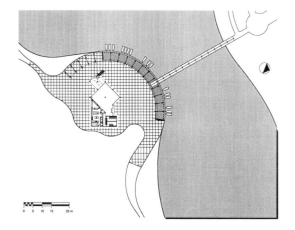

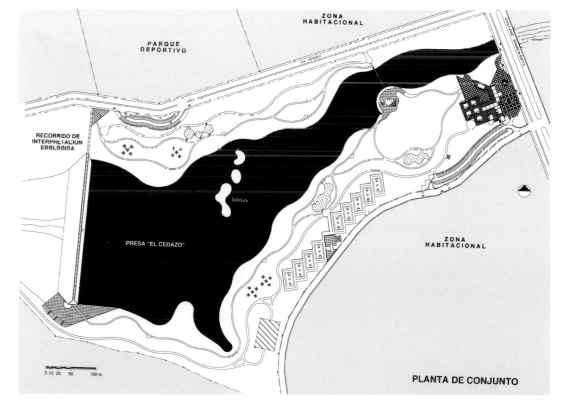

TOP LEFT: *Detail plan of cafeteria building and plaza in El Cedazo.*
LEFT: *Master plan of El Cedazo.*

PLANTA DE CONJUNTO

TOP LEFT, LEFT, AND OPPOSITE PAGE:
*Views of entry plaza and cultural cen-
ter buildings at El Cedazo.*

RIGHT: *View of main lake from rooftop cafeteria in El Cedazo.*

BELOW: *Detail of embarcadero canopy in El Cedazo.*

BELOW: *Lookout balcony from the retaining wall of the dam in El Cedazo.*
OPPOSITE PAGE: *Strolling path with pergola on top of dam in El Cedazo.*

BELOW: *Exercise area in Parque Mexico.*
OPPOSITE PAGE: *Amphitheater in Parque Mexico.*

TOP RIGHT: *Picnic areas and retaining wall in Parque Mexico.*
RIGHT: *View from the park's rooftop cafeteria.*
OPPOSITE PAGE: *Retaining dam and cascades in Parque Mexico.*

RIGHT: *Detail of stairs leading into*
the resevoir in Parque Mexico.

UNBUILT WORK

The Garden of Forgiveness, Beirut, Lebanon
Union Point Park, Oakland, California
Peralta Hacienda Historical Park, Oakland, California
Chiapas Natural History Institute, Chiapas

The Garden of Forgiveness Competition Proposal was Schjetnan's entry in an international design competition held in the year 2000 for a new park near Nejmeh Square in the center of Beirut. The site has both archaeological and current cultural significance: It contains Roman and medieval Arab ruins and is surrounded with religious institutions representing several of the faiths that exist in a state of chronic conflict in the Middle East. Physically, the site is equally complex. It is an elongated, folded rectangle that descends from street level to maximum depth of about five meters.

Schjetnan proposed dividing the park into two zones: the southern area dominated by the Roman remains and the northern space featuring new gardens organized around the Ottoman ruins. The gardens were imagined as a collage of local environments, from a cluster of Lebanese cedars evocative of high mountains to a grove of oaks and laurels indicative of lower elevations. These gardens were intended to suggest natural paradises, while nearby groves of olive, orange, or fig trees, along with grape vines and flower gardens, would allude to nature transformed by cultivation.

A loggia running along one side of the park would connect the two zones. It would function as an orientation and exhibition space called "The Gallery of Forgiveness" and display archaeological artifacts and historical materials relating to both the past and present-day clash of cultures in Beirut. The gallery would be enclosed and dark at one end but increasingly open and light toward the other, a structure intended to suggest hope and deliverance. A room reserved for contemplation would be located at the far end, overlooking a pool and the gardens. The loggia would thus function as a transitional space in literal and

ABOVE: *Existing site showing Roman ruins in the center of Beirut.*
OPPOSITE PAGE: *Detail of model of the Garden of Forgiveness in Beirut.*

figurative ways: between inside and outside and between past and future, but also between the historical and spiritual worlds—the former represented in the park's archeological zone, the latter evoked in its metaphors, common to Mediterranean cultures, of the garden as paradise.

In what was perhaps the proposal's most intriguing and provocative element, Schjetnan also proposed to use water on the sloping site to underscore his narrative of reconciliation. It would spring from spaces outside each of the five mosques and churches adjacent to the site: Al-Omari Mosque, St. Elias Catholic, St. George Orthodox, St. George Maronite, and a new mosque to be constructed adjacent to the Maronite church. Water would then descend into the park as small cascades and falls which would be transformed into a series of rills, channels, and pools. It would all come together in the main basin outside the final room in the loggia, the contemplative space. It would then circulate back to its sources. The constant flow of water, converging and dividing, might have provided a subtle but potent image of the idea of unification in difference that motivated the park design.

A network of elevated paths would have formed the park boundary. A bridge would cross the site at its narrowest point at street level; it would be as transparent as possible to intensify the view into the park. Circulation within the site would be oriented to different historic precedents. The entry from the north would be from present-day Avenue Foch, while the two main axes in the archaeological zone—running north-south and east-west—were determined by the Roman ruins. In between, the diagonal alignment in the garden area evokes the traces of medieval Arab occupation, when the orientation of the city was shifted northwest-southeast to align with its port. From the south, a ramp would lead down into the Roman ruins past the remains of imposing columns. A third entrance to the park would be found at the loggia, where a glass-enclosed elevator or a wide stair would lead down into a reception area and the exhibition space.

Materials for walls and walkways in the historic areas would be consistent with local uses, principally yellow sandstone. New construction, including bridges, the loggia, and ramps, would be in contemporary contrasting materials such as steel and aluminum. The

ABOVE: *Perspectives of orange orchard garden, loggia, and water garden and archaeological paths in the Garden of Forgiveness competition.*

park would have demonstrated sustainable principles, including the use of drought-tolerant Mediterranean species and a drip irrigation system. It would also incorporate water harvesting: rainwater that fell on the site would be collected in channels and purified in gravel filters and traps before entering the pool.

Schjetnan's proposal was not the competition's winning entry. Yet his message of reconciliation, hope, and tolerance is all the more compelling as a lasting peace in the Middle East seems more elusive than ever.

Union Point Park is Schjetnan's first project in the United States. Part of an extensive effort to create a system of parks and trails along Oakland's waterfront, Union Point is soon to be built on a nine-acre former industrial site. It will serve nearby Fruitvale and San Antonio neighborhoods, which have the city's highest concentration of children and greatest need for recreational open space. It will also provide public access to the Oakland estuary and ultimately be linked to the San Francisco Bay trail, which is proposed to circle the entire Bay.

A master plan for the park was developed by the landscape architecture firm EDAW through an elaborate community design process. The project was initiated through the joint efforts of the Oakland Department of Parks, Recreation and Cultural Services and a coalition of community groups called the Fruitvale Recreation and Open Space Initiative. The master plan proposed a shoreline trail; a series of earthen mounds to maximize views, provide shelter from traffic and wind, and create activity zones within the park; and several public art installations to aid interpretation of the park's cultural and natural features. It also incorporated a public boat landing and an existing marina.

Schjetnan's firm was retained for design development. The clients required them to maintain the basic structure of the master plan, including earth mounds, waterfront walk, playing fields, natural areas, and locations of entry points and service elements such as parking areas. The revised design (by GDU with Patillo & Garret of Oakland) intensified important elements from the original plan. For example, the mounds along the street edge

ABOVE: *Views of model for Union Point Park.*

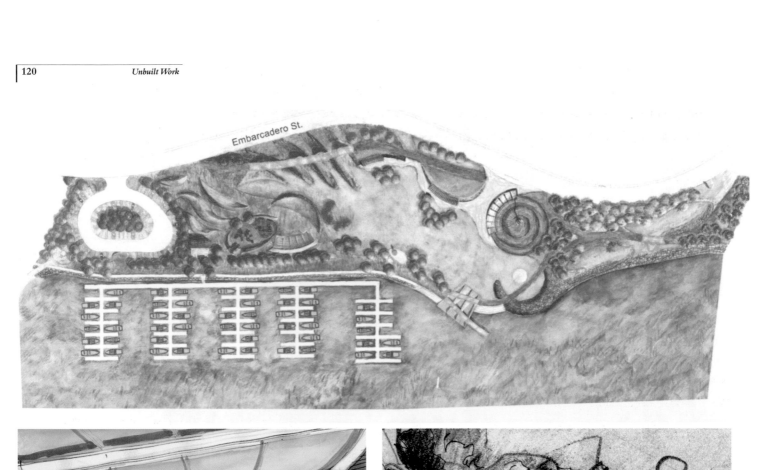

were reconfigured as a series of hills or dunes. While still providing shelter from traffic and wind, they are now perforated to permit elongated, framed glimpses into the park. Their summits will be linked by bridges, creating a pedestrian and bicycle trail with views toward the industrial city in one direction and the estuary in the other. One especially prominent mound named Union Point Hill will rise to a height of 21 feet; it will announce the park's major entrance. On top of this spiraling hill, a large inclined steel mast will support a steel and glass pergola suspended from cables over the entry plaza. The hill and mast will be illuminated at night as a beacon for this new public space.

The waterfront walk will connect marina facilities at one end of the park with with playing fields and natural areas at the other. Along this axis, intensity of use will diminish, from parking, playground, and picnic facilities at the north through less programmed playing field in the center and natural areas at the south. Midway, the trail will intersect with an environmental sculpture proposed by artist Ned Kahn to celebrate and interpret tidal and wave action. Picnic shelters modeled on the entry pergola and intended to give Union Point a clear visual identity will be dispersed around the park. Finally, the parking lot has been conceived as another entry plaza: an ellipse contained by trees featuring turf-block pavers to minimize storm water runoff and encourage infiltration. While Schjetnan's design language in this instance has been modified both by the existing master plan and the California context, his deft combination of lucid geometry with urban and environmental concerns is very much in evidence.

Peralta Hacienda Historical Park is situated in the heart of Oakland on the original location of Luis Peralta's ranch, the first non-indigenous settlement in San Francisco's East Bay. Peralta, a soldier, was given by the Spanish crown an 85,000 acre land grant—encompassing most of today's cities of Oakland, Berkeley, and San Leandro—and settled into a small adobe house on the site in 1820. The city of Oakland and a group of local residents organized as the Friends of Peralta Hacienda Historical Park have been working over the past several years to uncover the historical importance of the place and transform it into a community and recreation center for the Fruitvale district, a mixed community of Latinos,

BELOW: *Model view of Peralta Hacienda Historical Park.*
OPPOSITE PAGE: *Master plan and sketches of Union Point Park.*

African Americans, Asians, and whites.

Both the client and the designers (Schjetnan and GDU with Patillo & Garret of Oakland) have sought to interpret the social history and natural features of the site. Extensive archeological investigations have been conducted; many artifacts have been recovered. Peralta's 1820 and 1840 houses and the walls of their precinct are gone, but a street has been closed and a few modern houses have been bought and removed in order to uncover the surviving adobe footprints of these historic structures. The Peralta family's 1880s Victorian house has been restored to function as a site museum; a small adjacent 1890s house will be converted into a community center and supplemented by a new addition. Two other recent houses will be removed to open the park to the primary street, Coolidge Avenue, and to provide an open grass field for multipurpose recreation and informal games.

The park is naturally and distinctly divided into three areas: the upper and most urban edge along Coolidge Avenue; the historical precinct; and a heavily wooded creek, partially hidden and separated from the upper areas by a steep drop. The challenge of the project has been to acknowledge these distinct zones while weaving them together into a cohesive design. The recreational lawn, for example, will be divided from the historic precinct by a new adobe wall; both these areas are separated from the museum and community center buildings by an allée of pear trees. Yet this allée also serves to unify the park, providing a visual and physical link from the street to the historic core and suggesting the site's agricultural past. A second orchard will reconfigure the corner of Coolidge Avenue and Hyde Street; between the museum and community center an ethnobotanical garden will be planted, featuring exotic and indigenous food and medicinal plants important to early settlers.

The historical core has been designed in a contemporary Mexican idiom as a plaza or patio. The footprints of the two adobe houses will be covered with wood and metal ramadas. One of them will also contain an installation called the "urban book," a set of revolving panels relating the history of the area. The new adobe wall that frames this space will function as a backdrop for a stage area; to one side, a large table will be added, along

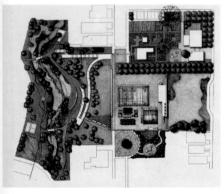

ABOVE: *Master plan for the Peralta Hacienda Historical Park.*

with an "aljibe" (well) and a "pila" (water basin), which are typical domestic elements of Mexican haciendas.

The link between the historic precinct and the creek area is established by a stair and a curving ramp. The creek itself has been reclaimed from a culvert and will be redesigned into pools with indigenous water plants and bracketed by shade gardens. Imagined as a place for interpretations of wetland ecology, the stream area will incorporate picnic facilities and a small amphitheater for children's classes. Play areas, located at the top of the slope adjacent to the historic core, will also be a prominent feature of the design.

Schjetnan's work at the **Chiapas Natural History Institute** in Tuxtla Gutierrez, Chiapas, was focused on reorganizing the public entrance and designing a new visitor center. A road that divided the park is to be closed and replaced with a pedestrian path, and a new entrance will be located along a peripheral street. A site for the new visitor center was selected in a nearby patch of dense rainforest that features a grove of majestic ficus and monkey ear trees.

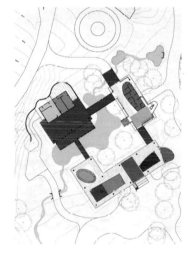

TOP: *Computer rendering of Zoomat's visitor center.*
ABOVE: *Plan of the new visitor center complex for Zoomat.*

The proposed facility will be composed of several pavilions elevated over a pond and wetlands. Flat roofs held aloft by slender columns will provide shelter from frequent rains, but walls for the most part will be absent, opening the structures to the surrounding tropical vegetation: only offices, shops, and an audiovisual theater will be enclosed. Wooden bridges will link the different pavilions over the water. Drawings suggest that the buildings might have the light, transparent character of pavilions in a Japanese garden. While the architectural idiom here is very different from that of the Museum of the Northern Cultures of Mexico, the Zoomat visitor center should achieve the same remarkable integration of building and landscape as Schjetnan's Chihuahua design.

FIRM PROFILE

Mario Schjetnan was born in Mexico City in 1945. He completed architecture studies at the National University of México (UNAM) in 1968. He obtained a Master's Degree in Landscape Architecture with emphasis in Urban Design at the University of California, Berkeley in 1970. In 1985 he was appointed Loeb Fellow in Advanced Environmental Studies at Harvard University Graduate School of Design. He received an Honorary PhD. from Universidad Autónoma de Nuevo León, México, 1995.

He is a founding partner, together with José Luis Pérez, of Grupo de Diseño Urbano (GDU), a firm established in 1977 in Mexico City with projects in landscape architecture, architecture and urban design. Schjetnan's work has been recognized by the American Society of Landscape Architects, with the President's Award of Excellence for Parque Tezozomoc; an Honor Award for Parque Historico Culhuacán and a Merit Design Award for Parque Ecológico Xochimilco, all of them in Mexico City. "Conceptually, Mario's work is not just about aesthetics. A lot of what he does is drawing from a very rich past and has to do with improving the well-being of people," wrote Bruce Sharky in Landscape Architecture Magazine. Schjetnan's work has been published in design magazines and books in Europe, Japan, Latin America, and the USA.
In 1992 Schjetnan's firm was distinguished with the International Critics Award in Architecture at the Biennial of Buenos Aires, Argentina, for an archaeological museum built in Paquimé, Chihuahua, Mexico. In 1996, Parque Ecológico Xochimilco was recognized with the distinguished Prince of Wales/Green Prize in Urban Design, given by Harvard University Graduate School of Design. In 1998, Schjetnan was again honored by ASLA with the President's Award of Excellence for Parque El Cedazo, Aguascalientes, Mexico, and with the Honor Award for the Golf Club in Malinalco, State of Mexico.

Schjetnan is a founding member and ex-president of the Mexican Society of Landscape Architects, Fellow of the National Academy of Architecture in Mexico, and Fellow of the American Society of Landscape Architects. In 1994 and 1998 he was visiting Design Critic at Harvard University Graduate School of Design. In 1997, the National Institute of Fine Arts of Mexico held a major exhibition of Schjetnan's work at the Palace of Fine Arts in Mexico City. Parallel with the exhibit a book was published on his work.

In spring 1999, Schjetnan was given the Federico Mariscal Chair for a series of lectures at the National Autonomous University of Mexico.

Since 1999, he has been Director and Professor in Practice at the School of Landscape Architecture, College of Planning, Architecture and Landscape Architecture, University of Arizona, Tucson.

PHOTO CREDITS

Tezozomoc
Michael Calderwood
Tom Lamb
Gabriel Figueroa
Boris de Swan

Culhuacán
Gabriel Figueroa
Jorge Sandoval
Gráfico: Brian L. Rothman

Casa Malinalco
Gabriel Figueroa

Cultural Mexiquense
Jorge Sandoval
Gonzalo Gómez Palacios

Xochimilco
Gabriel Figueroa
Michael Calderwood
Jorge Sandoval

Malinalco Golf Club
Tom Lamb
Arturo Zavala
Gabriel Figueroa

Paquimé
Gabriel Figueroa
Alfonso Muñoz

Parque México
Gabriel Figueroa

La Provincial Insurance
Alberto Moreno

El Cedazo Park
Gabriel Figueroa

Oficinas en el Parque
Gabriel Figueroa

Mario Schjetnan/gdu
Fernando Montes de Oca #4
Mexico City, D.F., Mexico 06140
Tel: 52 56 11 15/Fax: 52 86 10 13
correo@gdu.com.mx
www.gdu.com.mx

TECHNICAL DATA

Tezozomoc Park
Location: Azcapotzalco, Mexico City
Client: Azcapotzalco Delegation, Tulio Hernández and Sergio Martínez, delegates
Design and Construction Supervision: Mario Schjetnan Garduño, Jose Luis Pérez.
Collaborators: Jorge Calvillo
Lake and irrigation system: Mario Schjetnan Dantán +.
Area: 74.13 acres.
Construction finished: 1982.
Awards: President's Award of Excellence, 1989.
Honor Roll of Urban Parks from the American Society of Landscape Architects, Washington D,C,. U.S.A., 1995.

Malinalco House
Location: Malinalco, State of Mexico.
Client: Mrs. Romero de Schjetnan.
Design and Construction Supervision: Mario Schjetnan Garduño,
Collaborators: Jorge Calvillo, Manuel Peniche, and José Luis Pérez.
Construction finished: 1985
Area: 1,110 m2

Museum of Modern Art
Location: Toluca, State of Mexico
Client: Education and Culture Department of State of Mexico
Project and Direction: Mario Schjetnan Garduño, José Luis Pérez / Gonzalo Gomez Palacio
Advisor: Miriam Kaiser
Stone Mural: Luis Nishizawa
Construction finished: 1987
Awards: Prize from the International Academy of Architecture Critics, Buenos Aires Architecture Biennial, Argentina ,1991

Centro Cultural Mexiquense
Mexican Cultural Center
Location: Toluca, State of Mexico
Client: Education and Culture Department of State of Mexico
Project and Direction: Mario Schjetnan Garduño, José Luis Pérez
Project of the Museum of Arts and Crafts: Mario Schjetnan Garduño, José Luis Pérez, and Victor Monsivais
Project of History and Anthropology Museum: Pedro Ramirez Vazquez and Andres Giovanni García
Advisors : Mtra. Miriam Kaiser

Stone fountain: Luis Nishisawa and Mario Schjetnan
Construction finished: 1987
Awards: International Academy of Architecture Critics, Architecture Biennial of Buenos Aires , Argentina, 1991.

Culhuacán Historical Park
Location: Iztapalapa, Mexico City.
Client: Culhuacan Communitary Center, Instituto Nacional de Antropología e Historia (project director Cristina Payán)
Design and Construction Supervision: Mario Schjetnan Garduño, José Luis Pérez.
Archaeological Direction: Elsa Hernández, Archaeologist.
History Advisor: Juan Venegas, Historian.
Construction finished: 1988.
Area: 2.471 acres.
Awards: Gold medal at the second Mexican Architecture Biennial, 1992.
Honor Award from the American Society of Landscape Architects, Washington D.C., U.S.A., 1992.

Xochimilco Ecological Park
Location: Xochimilco, Mexico City
Client: Federal District Department.
Xochimilco Delegation
Project and Direction: Mario Schjetnan Garduño, José Luis Pérez / Grupo de Diseño Urbano.
Collaborators: Dr. Alejandro Novelo, Biólogo
Construction finished: 1993
Area: 667.17 acres
Awards: Honor Award from the American Society of Landscape Architects, Washington D, C, U.S.A., 1994. Prince of Wales/Green Prize in Urban Design, Harvard University GSD, 1996. Merit Design Award, The Waterfront Center, 1994

Malinalco Golf Club
Location: Malinalco, State of Mexico.
Client: Malinalco Golf Club, S.A. de C.V.
Design and Construction Supervision: Mario Schjetnan Garduño, José Luis Pérez.
Collaborators: Marco Arturo González.
Construction finished: 1993.
Area: 425.012 acres.
Awards: Honor Award from the American Society of Landscape Architects, Washington D,C, U.S.A., 1998. 1st. place Marble Architectural Awards from Internazionale Marmi e Macchine Carrara S.P.A., 2001.

La Provincial Insurance Company
Location: Coyoacan, Mexico City
Client: Grupo Nacional Provincial

Insurance Company
Design and Construction Supervision: Mario Schjetnan Garduño, José Luis Pérez.
Architectural Design: Augusto H. Alvarez and Associates.
Collaborators: José Luis Gómez Hidalgo, José Manuel Lira
Construction finished: 1994

Oficinas en el Parque Corporate Offices
Location: Monterrey, Nuevo León
Client: Desarrollos Inmobiliarios Delta (DID), Ing. Federico Garza Santos
Project and Direction: Arqs. Mario Schjetnan, José Luis Pérez / Grupo de Diseño Urbano S.C.
Architectural Design: DID/ Camargo Arquitectos.
Arq. José Angel Camargo, Arq. Juan Enrique López, Arq. Jaime Garza, Arq. Ricardo Torres
Sculpture Fountain: Mahia Biblos, Mario Schjetnan
Project Management: PLATE Administración de Proyectos.
Collaborators: Arq. Miguel Camacho (GDU), Arq. Alejandro Lira (GDU), Arq. José Luis Gómez.
Area: 7,300 m2 (Gardens and plazas)
Constrution finished: November 1999

Archaeological Museum of the Northern Cultures of Mexico
Location: Paquimé, Casas Grandes, Chihuahua, Mexico.
Client: Instituto Nacional de Antropología e Historia.
Design and Construction Supervision: Mario Schjetnan Garduño, José Luis Perez.
Archaeology and History Direction: Beatriz Braniff, Archaeologist.
Collaborators: Ricardo Sánchez, Socorro Alatorre, Arturo Sotomayor, José Luis Gómez, Pablo Romero, Alfredo Aranda, Francisco Ibañez and Salvador Escalante.
Museography: Jorge Agostoni, Architect/Museografica S.C.
Construction Finished: 1995.
Awards: Latin-American Prize from the Architecture Biennial Buenos Aires, Argentina, 1995.

Mexico Park
Location: Aguascalientes, Aguascalientes, Mexico
Client: Aguascalientes Government.
Fernándo Gómez Esparza, Mayor
Project and Direction: Mario Schjetnan Garduño, José Luis Pérez / Grupo de Diseño Urbano.
Collaborators: Marco Arturo González and Martín Andrade

Construction finished: 1995
Area: 42.007 acres

El Cedazo Recreational Park and Cultural Center
Location: Aguascalientes, Aguascalientes, México.
Client: Aguascalientes State Government.
Design and Construction Supervision: Mario Schjetnan and José Luis Pérez, Architects and Landscape Architects.
Collaborators: Marco Arturo González and Martín Andrade.
Construction finished: 1995.
Area: 158.144 acres.
Awards: President's Award of Excellence from The American Society of Landscape Architects.

The Garden Of Forgiveness
Location: Beirut, Lebanon
Client: Solidere
Design: Mario Schjetnan
Collaborators: Miguel Camacho, Alejandro Lira, Yara Sigler (GDU), Chuck Albanese (Professor of The University of Arizona) and Kelly Angel, Shane Chism, Nicolás García, Corey Haselhorst, Ellen Lazar and Emmanuel Torres (students of The University of Arizona).

Union Point Park
Location: Oakland, California
Client: The Unity Council
Design Lead: Mario Schjetnan (GDU)
Project Development: Chris Patillo (Patillo and Garrett Associates)
Collaborators: Alejandro Lira, Yara Sigler, Juan Carlos Guerra, Alma du Solier (GDU)

Hacienda Peralta Historical Park
Location: Oakland, California
Client: Friends of Hacienda Peralta Historical Park
Design Lead: Mario Schjetnan (GDU)
Project Development: Chris Patillo (Patillo and Garrett Associates)
Collaborators: Miguel Camacho, Alex Lira, Juan Carlos Guerra, Yara Sigler (GDU)

Zoomat
Location: Tuxtla Gutierrez, Chiapas
Client: Zoomat Instituto de Historia Natural del Gobierno del Estado de Chiapas
Design: Mario Schjetnan, Manuel Peniche, in collaboration with Augusto Alvarez (Augusto Alvarez y Asociados).
Collaborators: Juan Carlos Guerra, Edgar Paredes Marco Polo Fabián and Octavio Mendez (GDU)

SELECTED PROJECTS, AWARDS, AND BIBLIOGRAPHY

* Quinta Eugenia Housing Project. Mexico City, Mexico 111 dwellings (1977).
* San José del Cabo Tourist Development. Baja California, Mexico (1980).
* Urban Development Plan for the city of Merida. Yucatán, Mexico (1980).
* Bahías de Huatulco Environmental and Tourist Plan. Oaxaca, Mexico (1981).
* Tezozomoc Park. Azcapotzalco, Mexico City, Mexico 30 ha. (1981)
* Claustro de las Fuentes Cluster Development. Piedras Negras, Coahuila, Mexico, 88 houses (1982).
* MICARE Housing Project for Miners. Nava, Coahuila, Mexico, 1500 dwellings (1983).
* Mar de Cortés Cluster Development. La Paz, Baja California, Mexico, 9 dwellings (1983).
* Isla de Jaina Archaeological and Ecological Park. Campeche, Mexico 7000 ha. (1986).
* Marina Ixtapa Tourist Development, Preliminary Master Plan. Ixtapa, Guerrero, Mexico (1987).
* Mexican Cultural Center, Master Plan. Toluca, Mexico 170 ha. (1988).
* Museum of Modern Art. Toluca, Mexico (1988).
* Museum of Arts and Crafts. Toluca, Mexico (1988).
* Culhuacán Historical and Archaeological Park. Mexico City, Mexico 1 ha. (1989).
* Cerro de la Estrella National Park Master Plan. Iztapalapa, Mexico City, Mexico (1990).
* Terrazas del Bosque Housing Project. Preliminary Design. Cuajimalpa, Mexico City, Mexico (1990).
* El Canada Urban Park. Preliminary Master Plan. Monterrey, Nuevo León, Mexico (1990).
* National Medical Center Master Plan and Landscape Architecture. Mexico City, Mexico 15 ha. (1991).

* Cerro Prieto Industrial and Geothermal Park. Preliminary Master Plan. Baja California, Mexico (1991).
* Xochimilco Ecological Park. Recreational, Archaeological and Botanical Park. Mexico City, Mexico 267 ha. (1992).
* Arroyo Topo Chico Hydraulic, Ecological and Recreational Master Plan. Apodaca, Nuevo León, Mexico (1993).
* Ciudad Solidaridad Urban Center Master Plan and Landscape Architecture. Monterrey, Nuevo León, Mexico 700 ha. (1994).
* La Provincial Insurance Company. Landscape Architecture. Mexico City, Mexico (1994).
* Archaeological Museum for the Mayan Cultures Preliminary Design. Cancun, Quintana Roo, Mexico (1994).
* Golf Club in Malinalco Landscape Architecture. Malinalco, Mexico 170 ha (1994).
* El Cedazo Cultural and Recreational Park. Aguascalientes, Ags. Mexico. 40 ha. (1995).
* Park Mexico Recreational and Natural Park. Aguascalientes, Ags. Mexico 90 ha. (1995).
* Museum of the Northern Cultures. Paquimé, Casas Grandes, Chihuahua, Mexico (1995).
* Revised Master Plan of Mexico's National University Campus. Mexico City, Mexico, 700 ha. (1995).
* El Arco Housing Project for Miners. Preliminary Master Plan. Baja California Sur, Mexico (1996).
* Ethnobotanical and Historic Gardens. Preliminary Landscape Plan. Santo Domingo Cultural Center, Oaxaca, Mexico, 3 ha. (1996).
* El Cantil Quarry Park Master Plan. Mexico City, Mexico, 7 ha. (1996).
* Rancho Jaibas. Ecological Development Master Plan. Cala de Jaibas, Jalisco, Mexico, 168 ha. (1996).
* La Caridad Housing Project for Miners. Nacozari, Sonora, Mexico

(1997).
* IMMSA La Caridad Industrial Complex, Landscape Architecture. (1997).
* Marbella Urban and Touristic Development, Landscape Architecture. Viña del Mar, Chile, (1997).
* Ciudad Juárez Central Park, Cultural and Recreational Park. Ciudad Juárez, Chihuahua, Mexico, 58 ha. (1997).
* Valle Poniente Urban Development Master Plan. Monterrey, Nuevo León, Mexico. 350 ha. (1998).
* IMMSA Lead Plan. Urban Development Recycling Plan. Monterrey, Nuevo León, Mexico. 30 ha. (1998).
* Oficinas en el Parque Corporate Buildings, Landscape Architecture. Monterrey, Nuevo León, Mexico, (1988).
* Batopilas Urban Rehabilitation and Landscape Plan. Batopilas, Copper Canyon, Chihuahua, Mexico, (1988).
* Chihuahua City Cultural Corridor Landscape Plan. Chihuahua, Mexico (1988).
* El Zocalo. Urban and Landscape Design Competition. Mexico City, Mexico. Finalists (1998).
* Tlahuac Agricultural and Ecological District, Ecological and Landscape Restoration. Tlahuac, Mexico, 500 ha. (1999).
* Tlahuac. Agricultural and Ecological District, Tourist Pier and Plazas. Tlahuac, Mexico City. 500 ha. (1999).
* Tapachula Coffee Plantation Route, Ecotouristic Master Plan. Tapachula, Chiapas, Mexico. 3500 ha. (1999).
* Hacienda El Campanario Revised Urban Development Plan. Queretaro, Mexico. 500 ha. (1999).
* El Solar Mining Complex. Landscape Rehabilitation Plan. Taxco, Guerrero, Mexico, (1999).
* JVC Recreation and Office Park. Landscape Architecture. Guadalajara, Jalisco, Mexico. 300 ha. (1999).
* Siglum Office Building. Architecture.

Mexico City, Mexico (2000).
* Zoomat Zoo. Revised Master Plan. Tuxtla Gutierrez, Chiapas, Mexico. 120 ha. (2000).
* Zoomat Zoo. Preliminary Design of Visitor's Center. Tuxtla Gutierrez, Chiapas, Mexico, (2000).
* Union Point Park. Landscape Architecture and Architecture. Oakland, Caliofornia, USA. 9 acres (2000).
* Hacienda Peralta Historical Park. Landscape Architecture. Oakland, California, USA. 4 acres, (2000).
* The Garden of Forgiveness. International Landscape Design Competition. Beirut, Lebanon. Finalists (2000).
* Punta Brava Tourist Development. Urban Design and Landscape Architecture. Cancun, Quintana Roo, Mexico. 47 ha. (2001).

AWARDS

* Bradford Williams Medal, 1981. American Society of Landscape Architects.
* President's Award of Excellence. Parque Tezozomoc, 1989. American Society of Landscape Architects.
* Chalco Urban Center Solidarity Competition. Finalist 1990. Mexican Society of Architects.
* International Academy of Architects. Centro Cultural Mexiquense, 1991 Bienale de Arquitectura, Buenos Aires, Argentina.
* Honor Award Parque Histórico Culhuacán, 1992 American Society of Landscape Architects
* Gold Medal Parque Histórico Culhuacán, 1992 Mexican Federation of Architects, Bienale

* Design Award
   Parque Ecológico Xochimilco, 1994
   The Waterfront Center, Washington, USA
* Merit Design Award
   Parque Ecológico Xochimilco, 1994
   American Society of Landscape Architects
* Honor Roll of Urban Parks
   Parque Tezozomoc, 1995
   American Society of Landscape Architects
* Gran Premio Latinoamericano
   Museo de las Culturas del Norte, 1995
   Bienale de Arquitectura, Buenos Aires, Argentina
* Prince of Wales / Green Prize in Urban Design
   Parque Ecológico Xochimilco, 1996
   Harvard University, USA
* Honor Award
   Club de Golf Malinalco, 1998
   American Society of Landscape Architects
* Award of Excellence
   Parque El Cedazo, 1998
   American Society of Landscape Architects.
* First Prize in Urban Landscape
   Club de Golf Malinalco
   Marble Architectural Awards, 2001
   Carrara, Italy.

BIBLIOGRAPHY

* Alva Martínez, Ernesto (ed.) "Casa Cuarcatzintla", in La casa en la arquitectura mexicana, Mexico, Comex y Federación de Colegios de Arquitectos de la República Mexicana, 1995, pp. 138-139.
* ------, Color en la arquitectura mexicana, Mexico, Litoprocess, 1992, pp. 71, 83, 103, 169.
* ------, "Parque Histórico Culhuacán", in Restauración y remodelación en la arquitectura mexicana, Mexico, Comex y Federación de Colegios de Arquitectos de la República Mexicana, 1994, pp. 162-163.
* Larrosa, Manuel y Victor Jiménez, Arquitectura, Ciudad y Naturaleza, Mario Schjetnan / José Luis Pérez, México, Instituto Nacional de Antropología e Historia, 1997, pp. 70.
* "Architects of the United States of America", vol. 2, Australia, The Images Publishing Group, 1991, pp. 130-131.
* "Arquitectura e paisagem em centro cultural no Mexico", in Projeto, num. 120, Brasil, april 1989, pp. 60-65.
* Ashihara, Yoshinobu (ed.), World Collective Houses: 200 in the 20th century, Japan, Dayco Co. Ltd., 1990, pp. 295-298.
* Barragán, Luis, "Conversación de formas", interview by Mario Schjetnan, in Artes de México, num. 23, "En el mundo de Luis Barragán, special edition", Mexico, 1994, pp.74-77.
* Beardsley, John, "A word for landscape architecture", in Harvard Design Magazine, num. 12, Harvard University Graduate-School of Design, USA, fall 2000, pp. 56-63.
* "Casa en Malinalco", in 1990 Arquitectura Mexicana (Anuario, 10 obras), Mexico, november 1990, pp.38-41.
* Chávez, Daniel, "Tipologías Arquitectónicas Siglum Office Building", in ADI Arquitectura y Diseño Internacional, num.9, year 2, México, 2000, pp. 36-37.
* "Centro Cultural Mexiquense", in Proa, num. 4, Colombia (Monographies of Architecture / Latin American Architecture, 1980-1990), November 1991, pp. 60-61.
* "Centro Cultural Mexiquense: un proyecto integral de arquitectura, urbanismo y paisaje" in Proa, num. 377, Colombia, November 1988, pp.22-25.
* "Centro de Investigación para el mejoramiento del maíz y el trigo", in Cuadernos de Arquitectura y Conservación del Patrimonio Histórico/1968-78. Una década de arquitectura mexicana, num. 3, Mexico, SEP / INBA, may 1979, pp. 26-26.
* "Cinco Parques en uno", in Obras, num. 305, vol. XXV, México, May 1998, p.52
* "Club de Golf Malinalco: proyecto de arquitectura de paisaje" in Enlace, Arquitectura y Diseño, num. 4, year 6, Mexico, FCARM / CAM- SAM, April 1996, pp. 18-21.
* "Conjunto Quinta Eugenia", in Arquitectura/Mexico, num. 119, year 40, Mexico, 1978, pp.154-159.
* "Design Merit Award: Parque Ecológico Xochimilco, Mexico City, Mexico", in Landscape Architecture, num. 11, vol. 84, USA, November 1994, pp.79-80.
* "Honor Design award: El Club de Golf Malinalco", in Landscape Architecture, num.11, vol. 88, USA, November 1988, p.36.
* "El Cedazo: Diseño Integral", in Enlace arquitectura y diseño, num.2, year 9, Mexico, FCARM / CAM-SAM, February 1999, pp.74-81.
* Fieldhouse, Ken & Sheila Harvey (eds.), "Parque Tezozomoc", in Landscape Design and International Survey, London, Kalman King Press, pp.28-29.
* García Coll, Julio y Mario Schjetnan, Mexico Urbano, Mexico, Fondo de Cultura Económica, 1975.
* Glusberg, Jorge, "Arquitectura y naturaleza en el Parque Ecológico Xochimilco", in La Revista, num. 459, Argentina, April 1994, pp.63-64.
* González, Isaura, "Un nuevo símbolo de identidad en avenida Insurgentes, Siglum Office Building", in ADI Arquitectura y Diseño Internacional, num. 9, year 2, México, 2000, pp. 36-37.
* "Groupe d'habitations, Quinta Eugenia, Mexico, 1977", in Techniques & architecture, num. 30, France, June/July 1978, pp. 129, 144, 145.
* Holden, Robert, "Parque Ecológico Xochimilco" in Diseño del espacio público internacional, Barcelona, Gustavo Gili Editores, 1996, pp.94-97.
* Jellicoe, Geoffrey and Susan Jellicoe, "Parque Tezozomoc", in The Landscape of man, New York, The Viking Press, 1994, pp.375.
* Karasov, Deborah, "Xochimilco: where myth and memory meet", in Public Art Review, num. 2, vol 10, issue 20, USA, spring-summer 1999, pp.19-22.
* Kassner, Lilly, "El Centro Cultural Mexiquense", in Mexico en el Arte, num. 18, Mexico, INBA, fall 1987, pp.69-71.
* ----- "Premio internacional de arquitectura de paisaje", in Arte en Colombia, num.42, Colombia, Internacional, december 1989, pp.44-45.
* Kolstad Kirsten, "Parque Ecológico Xochimilco", in Arkitektnytt, num. 3, Oslo, February 1995, pp. 1, 40-41.
* Leñero Elu, Marisa and Xavier Guzmán Urbuiola, "El Parque Tezozomoc: naturaleza correletiva", in Universidad de Mexico, num. 479, vol. XLV, Mexico, UNAM, December 1990, pp.33-36.
* Meier, Rudolf, "Xochimilco, Parque Ecológico Xochimilco", in Garten + Landschaft, num. 6, Germany, 1996, pp. 11-15.
* "Museo de las Culturas del Norte", in ARQ. Chile, num. 34, Santiago de Chile, Escuela de Arquitectura Pontificia-Universidad Católica de Chile, December, 1996, pp. 66-67.
* "Museo de las Culturas del Norte", in Tostem View, num. 59, Japan, May 1996, pp. 2, 9.
* "News", in Landscape Architecture, num. 12, vol. 81, USA, December 1991, p.20.
* "Novedades Mexicanas: arquitectura, ciudad y naturaleza", in Ambiente, Etica y estética para el ambiente construido, year XXIII, Argentina, CEPA, November 1999, pp. 10-16.
* "Obra del mes: el Centro Cultural Mexiquense", in Obras, Mexico, August 1987, pp. 11-23.
* "Obra del mes: la imagen del siglo XXI", in Obras, num. 233, vol. XXIV, Mexico, May 1992, pp.10-23.
* "Parc Ecologique de Xochimilco, México", in L'architecture d'aujourd'hui, France, September-October 1999, pp.31-34.
* "Parque Ecológico de Xochimilco", in Arquitectura, num.10, Mexico, May 1994, pp.52-57.
* "Parque Ecológico Xochimilco: un acierto político y de arquitectura del paisaje", in Entorno Inmobiliario, num.6, Mexico, November-December 1993, pp. 5-9.
* "Parque natural y embarcadero Lago de los reyes", in Enlace Arquitectura y Diseño, num. 1, year 10, México, FCARM / CAM-SAM, January 2000, pp. 106-107.
* "Parque Histórico Culhuacán: Honor Award", in Landscape Architecture, USA, November 1992, p. 64.
* "Parque Histórico Culhuacán", in Anuario de Arquitectura 1991, special publication, Mexico, 1991, pp.28-31.
* "Parque Histórico Culhuacán", in Arquitectura del Paisaje, num. 7,

Colombia, May/July 1991, pp-6-7.
* "Parque infantil y deportivo Cove", in Arquitectura, num. 4, Mexico, winter 1992, pp.58-59.
* "Parque Mexico", in Arquitectura y Sociedad, num. 32, year XXXVIII, Mexico, 1983, pp.9-13.
* "Parque México", in Cuarta reseña de arquitectura mexicana, México, OTIS, 1999, pp.120-123.
* "Parque recreativo y cultural Tezozomoc-Azcapotzalco", in Arquitectura del paisaje, num.7, Colombia, May / July 1991, pp.2-5.
* "Parque Tezozomoc", in Landscape Architecture, num.9, vol. 79, USA, November 1989, pp.48-51.
* "Parque Tezozomoc", in Proa, num.4, Colombia (Monographies in Architecture / Latin American architecture, 1980-1990), november 1991, p. 62.
* "Parque Tezozomoc-Azcapotzalco", in Arquitectura y Sociedad, num. 32, year XXXVIII, Mexico, 1983, pp.14-16.
* "Plaza Miguel Hidalgo", in Process Architecture, num.39, Japan, Modern Mexican Architecture, July 1983, pp.100-101.
* Plazola, Guillermo, "Parque Xochimilco", in 50 años de arquitectura mexicana 1948-1988, México, Union Internacional de Arquitectos, 1999, pp. 126-128.
* -----, "Museo de las Culturas del Norte", in Enciclopedia de Arquitectura, México, Plazola Editores SA de CV, 1994, pp.404-405.
* -----, "Centro Médico Nacional siglo XXI", in Encyclopedia de Arquitectura, México, Plazola Editores SA de CV, 1994, pp. 281-282.
* "Premio Internacional de Arquitectura de paisaje a Schjetnan y Pérez", in Arquine, México, spring 1999, pp.11-12.
* "President's award of excellence: Parque El Cedazo", in Landscape Architecture, num. 11, vol. 88, USA, November 1998. p.36.
* "Proyecto de desarrollo urbano y vivienda media popular, Ciudad Solidaridad, Monterrey", in Construcción y Tecnología, num. 76, vol. VII, Mexico, September 1994, pp.14-15.
* Ramírez, David, "Parque Histórico Culhuacán", in Zona Verde, Spain, December 1989, pp.19-22.

* Rigby, D., "Parque Ecológico Xochimilco", in The New Waterfront, USA, The Waterfront Center / Mc Graw-Hill, 1996.
* Roca, Miguel Angel (ed.), "Parque Ecológico Xochimilco, Parque Histórico Culhuac·n y Centro Cultural Mexiquense", in The Architecture of Latin America, London, Academy Editions, 1995, pp. 1, 114-119.
* Schjetnan, Mario, "Un paisaje urbano es el reflejo de una sociedad", interview by Consuelo González Avilez, in Construcción y tecnología, num.38, vol. IV, Mexico, July 1991, pp.20-23.
* -----, "Ciudad de Mexico 2010:recuperación de su habitabilidad", in Ciencia, Arte y Cultura, num.1, Mexico, Instituto Politécnico Nacional, October-December 1990, pp-6-15.
* -----, "Ciudad y naturaleza hacia fines del siglo XX", in ARQ. Chile, num.34, Santiago de Chile, Escuela de Arquitectura Pontificia/ Universidad Catulica de Chile, December 1996.
* -----, "El arte del paisaje", in Artes de MÈxico, num. 15, special edition, Mexico, 1993, pp.10-15.
* -----, "Il parco ecológico di Xochimilco", in Lotus International, num.91, Milan, Electa, November 1996, pp.110-131.
* -----, "Linking 14 km of Hotels by Bikeway", in Landscape Architecture, USA, 1977, pp. 497-499.
* -----, "Luis Barrag·n: the Influential Lyricist of Mexican Culture", in Landscape Architecture, USA, January 1982, pp.68-75.
* -----, "Monumental Spaces", in Landscape Architecture, num. 6, vol. 6, USA, August 1989, pp. 50-53.

* -----, "Myth, History and Culture: Parque Tezozomoc", in Landscape Architecture, num.2, vol.74, USA, March / April 1984, pp.75-79.
* -----, "Parque Recreativo y Centro Cultural El Cedazo", in Enlace, Arquitectura y Diesño, year 7, Mexico, FCARM / CAM-SAM, January 1997, pp. 68-75.
* -----, "Parque Tezozomoc", in Zona Verde, Spain, December 1989, pp.14-18.
* -----, "Tezozomoc: un ejemplo de parque urbano", in Tecnología y Arquitectura, num.8, Spain, January 1990, pp. 102-107.

* -----, "The Resurrection of Xochimiclo", in Alex Krieger (ed.), Mexico City, 1996, Veronica Rudge Green Prize in Urban Design. The Restoration of Mexico City and the Ecological Restoration of the District of Xochimilco, USA, Harvard University- Graduate School of Design, 1996, pp. 1 -56.
* -----, "The Cancun Strip: Mexico's Bid for Touristic Dollars", in Landscape Architecture, USA, 1977, pp. 491-496.
* -----, "Trilogía rota: arquitectura, ciudad y naturaleza", in Construcción y Tecnología, num. 50, vol. V, Mexico, July 1992, pp. 35-36.
* -----, "Ecatepec, El Albarradón de Nezahualcóyotl" in Ecatepec, México: rescate de mito, historia y paisaje. Proyecto de un parque lineal ecológico, arqueológico, recreativo y cultural, USA, Harvard University-Graduate School of Design, fall 1994.
* -----, "Lage, raum, stein", in Garten + Landschaft, Germany, february 1999, pp. 13-16.
* Schjetnan, Mario, "Entrevista a Mario Schjetnan", interview by Alejandro Cabeza, in Bitacora, México, UNAM, winter 2000, pp. 28-35.
* Schjetnan, Mario, José Luis Pérez, Anibal Figueroa et al., Criterios de adecuación bioclimática en la arquitectura, México, IMSS, 1990.
* Schjetnan, Mario, Manuel Peniche y Jorge Calvillo, Principios de diseño urbano ambiental, México, Concepto, 1984.
* Seóa y trazo: 10 años del Centro Cultural Mexiquense, num. 9, year 3, special edition, Toluca, México, Instituto Mexiquense de Cultura, May 1997.
* Swan, Boris, "Tezozomoc: un parque secreto", in México Desconocido, num. 159, year XIII, México, May 1990, pp.25-27.
* Thompson, J. William, "Aztec Revival", in Landscape Architecture, num. 4, vol. 84, USA, April 1994, pp.62-65.
* -----, "Cultural Simplicity", in Garden Design, USA, August 1992, pp.52-55.
* -----, "Landscape as Myth and Culture", in Landscape Architecture, num. 1, vol. 84, USA, January 1994, pp. 72-75.

* -----, "Dual Gesture", in Landscape Architecture, num. 10, vol. 88, USA, October 1998, pp. 105-113.
* Toca, Antonio y Anibal Figueroa, "Conjunto Claustro Las Fuentes", in Nueva Arquitectura Mexicana, Mexico, Ediciones Gili, 1991, pp. 90-93.
* -----, "Parque Tezozomoc-Azcapotzalco", in Nueva Arquitectura Mexicana, México, Ediciones Gili, 1991, pp. 84-89.
* "Unidad Habitacional Quinta Eugenia", in Process Architecture, num.39, Japan, Modern Mexican Architecture, July 1983, pp. 97-99.
* Waisman, Marina, "El misterio de la escala", in Summa, num.5, Argentina, Centro Cultural Mexiquense, 1992.
* Wyman Louise, "A critical regionalist, Mario Schjetnan for Grupo de DiseÒo Urbano", in Landscape Design, London, Journal of the Royal Institute of British Landscape Architects, February 1997, pp.10-14.